Maynooth Studies in Local History: Number 93

The Donegal Plantation and the Tír Chonaill Irish, 1610–1710

Darren McGettigan

FOUR COURTS PRESS

Set in 10pt on 12pt Bembo by
Carrigboy Typesetting Services for
FOUR COURTS PRESS LTD
7 Malpas Street, Dublin 8, Ireland
www.fourcourtspress.ie
and in North America for
FOUR COURTS PRESS
c/o ISBS, 920 N.E. 58th Avenue, Suite 300, Portland, OR 97213.

ISBN 978–1–84682–264–3

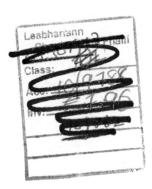

Printed in Scotland by
Thomson Litho, Glasgow.

The Donegal Plantation and the Tír Chonaill Irish, 1610–1710

Maynooth Studies in Local History

SERIES EDITOR Raymond Gillespie

This volume is one of six short books published in the Maynooth Studies in Local History series in 2010. Like over 85 of their predecessors they range widely over the local experience in the Irish past. That local experience is presented in the complex social world of which it is part, from the world of the dispossessed Irish in 17th-century Donegal to political events in 1830s Carlow; from the luxury of the early 19th-century Dublin middle class to the poverty of the Famine in Tipperary; and from the political activists in Kimmage in 1916 to those who suffered in a different sort of war as their homes were bombed in South Circular Road in 1941. These local experiences cannot be a simple chronicling of events relating to an area within administrative or geographically determined boundaries since understanding the local world presents much more complex challenges for the historian. It is a reconstruction of the socially diverse worlds of poor and rich as well as those who took very different positions on the political issues that preoccupied the local societies of Ireland. Reconstructing such diverse local worlds relies on understanding of what the people of the different communities that made up the localities of Ireland had in common and what drove them apart. Understanding the assumptions, often unspoken, around which these local societies operated is the key to recreating the world of the Irish past and reconstructing the way in which those who inhabited those worlds lived their daily lives. As such, studies such as those presented in these short books, together with their predecessors, are at the forefront of Irish historical research and represent some of the most innovative and exciting work being undertaken in Irish history today. They also provide models which others can follow up and adapt in their own studies of the Irish past. In such ways will we understand better the regional diversity of Ireland and the social and cultural basis for that diversity. If they also convey something of the vibrancy and excitement of the world of Irish local history today they will have achieved at least some of their purpose.

Contents

Acknowledgments

First and foremost I would like to express my very grateful thanks to my parents Eamonn and May. Without their love and support this book would not have been written. I would also very much like to thank the rest of my family, my brothers and sisters, Paul, Teresa, Anna and William, and my aunt Ann, and especially the new additions to the family since my last book, my niece Solas and new nephew Daniel who was born in 2010. I also wish to thank all my friends for their companionship over the time I was researching and writing this book, especially my friends Denis Teevan, Tony and Emily McCormack and his parents, Paul and Gillian McGuill, Ronan and Caroline LeLu and their young family, Emmett O'Byrne, Terry Clavin, Gavin Slattery and Joe and Estefania McNabb whose new baby Thomas also arrived in 2010. Others I would like to thank include my aunt and uncle, Frank and Marion McGettigan and my uncle Stephen Hunter and his family. For their assistance while researching and writing this book I would like to thank Professor Raymond Gillespie for agreeing to include my research as part of this year's Maynooth Studies in Local History series, and the staff of Four Courts Press for seeing it through publication. I also wish to thank my PhD supervisor, Dr Tadhg Ó hAnnracháin for his assistance, and Seamus Helferty, principal archivist of the UCD archives and the UCD-OFM Partnership for permission to reproduce images of two letters from the Wadding Papers which I have used for the cover and as an illustration in my book. I also would like to thank the very helpful staff of the James Joyce Library at UCD, the Trinity College Dublin Manuscript Library, Marsh's Library Dublin, the National Library of Ireland, particularly the manuscript library, the staff of the National Archives of Ireland, the National Archives, Kew, London, and also of the Public Record Office of Northern Ireland. Thanks are also due to the Vatican Library for permission to reproduce fig. 4 from the Barberini MSS. Finally I would again like to express my heartfelt appreciation to my extended family in Co. Donegal who made me feel totally welcome every time I visited Tír Chonaill.

Introduction: Co. Donegal in 1610

Donegal is the westernmost county in the province of Ulster. It was shired by Queen Elizabeth's administration in 1585 and the current county boundaries were finalized in the early 17th century. The general area of the county follows that of the Gaelic lordship of Tír Chonaill, the patrimony of the O'Donnell family, particularly when it was at its greatest extent from around 1450 to 1603. Indeed, the older medieval lordship of Tír Chonaill which was a very ancient territory, covered most of the south and west of the modern county. Donegal is a mountainous county, with good areas of land along its eastern and southern borders. There are some smaller fertile pockets interspersed among the central Bluestack and Derryveagh Mountains, and many islands off the western coast, some of which are quite large. There is one major north-south route through the mountains, the pass of Bearnas Mór and in 1610 there was one large forested district in Co. Donegal, Ceann Maghair on Mulroy Bay which covered 10 townlands.[1] In 1608 Lord Deputy Chichester described the Derryveagh Mountains as: 'That part of Tír Chonaill which containeth also a great circuit, is the most barren, uncouth and desolate country ... that is to be seen, fit only to confine rebels and ill spirits into'.[2] Sir Thomas Ridgeway, the Irish Treasurer also left a description of Glenveagh dating from 1608. He states that the valley was: 'closed in with two very steep and downright mountains, on the one side, three quarters of a mile, and on the other side a quarter of a mile high: one third part of the glen being nothing but lough water, another third part bog, which begins where the water ends. The other third part skirted all in length, with thick and short wood'.[3]

County Donegal was a territory still feeling the damaging effects of the Nine Years War – a major conflict fought on the island of Ireland between 1594 and 1603. The lordship of Tír Chonaill had been one of the most important confederate strongholds under the young chieftain, Red Hugh O'Donnell, who ruled Donegal from 1592 to 1602. There were two main periods of destruction in the O'Donnell lordship. The first was the late 1580s and early 1590s when the O'Donnell nobles demolished their own castles to prevent English captains garrisoning them.[4] The second was from May 1600 when a large English force landed at Derry and from there fanned out into the surrounding territories with the assistance of some disaffected local nobles. The destruction in Co. Donegal during the years 1600–2 was very extensive. Again many of the Gaelic nobles in the north of the county destroyed their own castles to prevent the English seizing them. Churches were also burned by the English and thousands of cattle and sheep seized. English soldiers garrisoned the Franciscan monastery of Donegal and the abbey at Rathmullan, the former being blown up by an explosion of gunpowder in September 1601 and almost completely destroyed. One of the worst incidents of the war occurred when an English force got onto Inch Island in Lough Swilly which 'had in it between four and 500 Irish houses, it was a magazine for O'Doherty's corn, and was now burned and spoiled by the garrison of Derry which brought away 2,000 sheep, 200 garrans, 250 cows [and] slew the people being near 150 and burned the corn being adjudged worth the value of £3,000'.[5] Similarly in the spring of 1602 when Niall Garbh O'Donnell took the confederate stronghold of Ballyshannon castle, having bombarded it with a demi cannon, the English and their Gaelic allies 'put ... to death ... the women and boys, in number 300', the garrison having fled during the night 'seeing that there was no assistance or relief at hand'.[6]

There was also a major localized rebellion in north Donegal in 1608 when Sir Cahir O'Doherty, the lord of Inishowen, sacked and burned the new town of Derry. O'Doherty subsequently based himself in the valley of Glenveagh in the heart of the Derryveagh Mountains. However, he was killed soon after at the battle of Kilmacrennan. Again there was much destruction in Co. Donegal during this rebellion. Burt castle in Inishowen, Lough Gartan crannog, Doe castle and Tory Island castle were all taken by Lord Deputy Chichester's forces, with the garrisons of Lough Gartan and Tory Island being brutally induced to kill each other.[7] The outbreak of the 1608 rebellion led to anarchy in Co. Donegal with some nobles raiding their more vulnerable neighbours, ransacking the houses of their tenants and stealing their cattle and sheep.[8] Over 20 people were executed at Lifford in the aftermath of O'Doherty's revolt which saw British forces campaign in such isolated areas as the islands off the western coastline of Donegal which had probably never seen the arrival of soldiers from England or Scotland before.

In the aftermath of the Nine Years War, Red Hugh O'Donnell's brother Rory was created the first earl of Tír Chonaill by the new British king James I. Rory surrendered in December 1602, being allowed to return to Tír Chonaill with his adherents in February 1603 and soon after was created earl. It was not long before Earl Rory was commenting on the destruction and depopulation visited on Co. Donegal by the Nine Years War. In 1605 the earl wrote that most of his land was 'waste by reason that the ancient inhabitants dwell in other places, having had wrongs daily preferred them'.[9] Rory indicated in 1606 that 'His poverty is so great, by reason of his unpeopled country, that he must be a suitor for Salisbury's favour'.[10] In 1625–6, 18 of 30 quarters in the territory of Clanelly lying between the rivers Swilly and Leannan were still 'lying waste',[11] while Bishop Andrew Knox of Raphoe commented that when he arrived in Donegal in 1611 his bishopric was 'waste and without inhabitants' and that in 1632 some areas such as Gartan were still

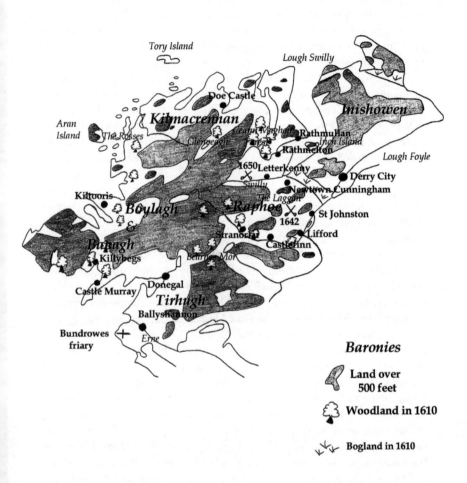

Tory Island

Lough Swilly

Doe Castle

Inishowen

Aran
Island

Kilmacrennan

The Rosses

Ceann Maghair

Rathmullan

Clongeagh

Forest

Inch Island

Rathmelton

Lough Foyle

1650 Letterkenny

Derry City

Swilly

Newtown Cunningham

The Laggan

Kiltooris

Boylagh

Raphoe

St Johnston

1642

Banagh

Stranorlar

Lifford

Killybegs

Beirnes Mór

Castlefinn

Castle Murray

Donegal

Tirhugh

Ballyshannon

Bundrowes
friary

Erne

Baronies

Land over
500 feet

Woodland in 1610

Bogland in 1610

1 Co. Donegal, 1610–1710

'the worst land in the diocese ... and part of it lately lay waste'.[12] However, this is to give a false picture of the lordship of Tír Chonaill. The O'Donnell lordship in its heyday was large, well governed and prosperous, with a small town at Donegal and a lucrative fishing industry in the seas offshore. Nevertheless, there had been an increasing level of violence in the lordship of Tír Chonaill even before the Nine Years War, and by 1610 the county did present to the outside observer a ruined and depopulated state.

For a variety of reasons Rory O'Donnell's finances rapidly deteriorated during the time of his earldom from 1603 to 1607. Vital fertile areas had been exempted from his patent (the document recording the grant of Tír Chonaill to Rory from the king) as had the O'Doherty lordship of Inishowen and the lordship of the O'Donnells of Castlefinn.[13] The valuable fisheries of the lordship of Tír Chonaill were also taken from the earl. These were worth well over £1,000 per annum.[14] By 1606 the earl wrote to James I that 'seeing his estate plunged into so deep a pit of misery, as he shames to express before his Majesty',[15] a number of people having 'sucked all the wealth of that land which his Highness bestowed on me this three years passed to themselves'.[16] County Donegal was very lawless in the years following the end of the Nine Years War in 1603. The earl's rival Niall Garbh O'Donnell, the lord of Glenfinn, never settled down under his kinsman's rule. In 1603 Niall Garbh had himself inaugurated the O'Donnell chieftain, but then had to flee to the woods of Ceann Maghair as the earl and the British authorities in the county were sent to arrest him.[17] The Annals of the Four Masters record that 'vast numbers' of Niall Garbh's followers 'died of cold and famine' when the earl and the English seized their cattle herds. The next year Niall Garbh in turn exploited the absence of the earl, who was away on business, and 'possessed himself of the tenants and herds of cattle' belonging to Rory until he had 'grown so strong as the earl ... holds it not safe to return thither'.[18] The extortions of woodkerne (Gaelic bandits), were again a serious problem in Donegal as were the depredations of the British garrisons in the county, which were the original cause of the Nine Years War in Tír Chonaill. Soldiers from Derry, Lifford and Ballyshannon seized cattle, sheep, pigs, plough horses and women from the earl's tenants, creating great hardship and resentment. The worst incident in a campaign by the garrison troops 'when they committed many rapes and used many extortions' was the rape of 'a young maiden of the age of 11 years' who was held down by two soldiers while a Captain Ellis 'satisfied his lascivious desires'. When the earl attempted to defend his tenants he was attacked himself. Five soldiers broke into the earl's house to take the earl's carriage horses and ran one of his servants through with a pike or sword when the boy refused to assist them. An attempt to murder O'Donnell was also made when he was on a journey to the Pale through Connacht. Rory was set upon in Boyle, Co. Roscommon by the constable and 20 soldiers, and only managed to save himself by barricading himself into a house and defending it all night with his three servants. Rory was rescued the next morning 'by the country folk which conveyed him safely out of the town'.[19]

The level of post-war violence in Co. Donegal also destroyed the earl's attempted land reforms. As Hugh O'Neill, earl of Tyrone, was to do in his own lordship, O'Donnell made a determined effort to restore the finances of his earldom by making new arrangements with his sub-chieftains. Due to his patent of 1604 Rory controlled most of the county in his own right in a different way to the traditional lordship of the O'Donnell lord of Tír Chonaill. It was later claimed that in 1604: 'Diverse gentlemen claiming freehold in ye county as namely the three septs of the McSweeneys, Banagh, Fanad and Doe, O'Boyle and O'Gallagher, but these men past over their rights (if any they had) to the earl (as is said) which he got from them, contentiously and by unworthy means'.[20] This created a great deal of resentment as the McSweeneys of Doe and Fanad and one of the earl's first cousins, Caffar Óg O'Donnell, violently opposed the earl's land reforms. When the earl seized Doe castle from the McSweeneys of Doe he had to have the Gaelic noble Owen Óg McSweeney executed for his opposition. Even then a Niall McSweeney drove the earl's constable out of the castle 'by means whereof the earl lost the rent of 60 quarters of land for the space of one year and a half'.[21] It is also recorded that there was trouble amongst the McSweeneys of Fanad where the prominent noble Walter McSweeney 'and others of the sept of Fanad, opposed themselves against the grant'.[22] In January 1607 Caffar Óg O'Donnell and Niall McSweeney launched what was called 'a kind of rebellion' against the earl centred on Doe castle and the woods of Ceann Maghair.[23] Having about 60 men, O'Donnell and McSweeney plundered and killed people loyal to the earl in the surrounding area.[24] Earl Rory, Sir Richard Hansard and Niall Garbh O'Donnell were ordered by the British authorities to suppress the outbreak, which they did successfully. Niall Garbh was almost killed as he stormed Doe castle.[25] In the end Caffar Óg O'Donnell fled to the Hebrides 'with 30 men in company well appointed after their fashion'.[26]

By the beginning of 1607, however, the earl's finances were in a critical mess. A year later in October 1608 Lord Deputy Chichester was to write that Tír Chonaill 'hath been so bangled by the earl of Tír Chonaill by sales, mortgages, and underhand conveyances that I can make no certain demonstration thereof'.[27] Rory O'Donnell mortgaged much land in Cinél Móen, including his mother Ineen Dubh's estate of 15 quarters of land in Tír Breasail and also the O'Friel termon lands in the Kilmacrennan area, to Alderman Nicholas Weston, a merchant from Dublin.[28] Additional lands were granted to a second Dublin merchant, Patrick Conley, and the earl also granted Doe castle to a third Dublin merchant John Arthur in 1607. Conley later alleged that the earl owed him over £1,770 pounds for the mortgage and lease of a further 64 quarters of land.[29] By the time of the departure of O'Donnell in September 1607 in the flight of the earls, the finances and system of land ownership in

Co. Donegal was very confused. Merchants claimed mortgages and loans and the earl himself must have been close to bankruptcy. As Nicholas Canny put it 'reading his catalogue of woes, one is left with the impression that flight might have come as a pleasant relief to him after years of bickering'.[30] In the end Rory O'Donnell was fortunate to get away when the son of McSweeney Fanad sent 'a party of the people of the district' who 'came upon them in pursuit. They fought with one another'.[31] Niall Garbh O'Donnell also stated that 'he pursued them when they went away'.[32] Rory probably left Donegal to secure a Spanish pension or military post in Flanders. He died, however, in 1608 in Rome.

Although the British administration in Ireland issued a proclamation 'to the inhabitants of Tyrone and Tír Chonaill' stating that 'inhabitants ... will not be disturbed in the possession of their lands as long as they are peaceable',[33] the flight of the earls left a dangerous vacuum in Co. Donegal. This vacuum was utilized by the earl's rival Niall Garbh O'Donnell, who exploited younger men such as Sir Cahir O'Doherty, the lord of Inishowen for his own ends. Niall Garbh O'Donnell never took out a patent for his very extensive lands in Glenfinn 'expecting greater quantities and pretending title to the whole country, which I think will hardly satisfy his ambition', as Lord Deputy Chichester put it.[34] When Cahir O'Doherty was physically assaulted by Governor Paulet, O'Donnell exploited the younger man's anger and urged him to gain revenge. O'Doherty proceeded to burn Derry to the ground but his rebellion was a disaster and he was killed soon after. Niall Garbh hoped to engineer a situation whereby the English administration in Ireland would have to turn to him to restore law and order in Co. Donegal by appointing him lord of Tír Chonaill. However, O'Donnell had not counted on O'Doherty's sudden death and Lord Deputy Chichester's ruthless suppression of the rebellion. In fact Niall Garbh was implicated in sending a band of woodkerne to help storm Derry and with continuing to send intelligence to O'Doherty.[35] Lord Deputy Chichester used the outbreak of the rebellion to arrest Niall Garbh, his brothers Hugh Boy and Donal, his son Neachtan and Caffar Óg O'Donnell and also seized a young infant nephew of the earl of Tír Chonaill who had been left behind after the flight of the earls. This decimated the leadership of the O'Donnell family and eliminated any potential focus of opposition to the future plantation.[36]

Even before the beginning of the official plantation in Co. Donegal in 1610, there were new British landlords in the county and the nature of landholding was rapidly changing. In 1605 the Scottish cleric George Montgomery was appointed Protestant bishop of the three dioceses of Derry, Clogher and Raphoe by King James I.[37] Immediately on arriving in Ulster Montgomery began to investigate the lands of his dioceses and laid claim to any episcopal land which had been alienated from the church by the local families over the centuries. There was much of this type of land in Co. Donegal and in an

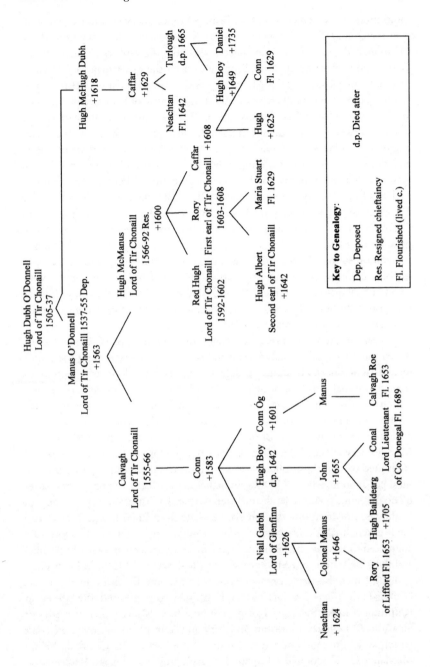

2 Genealogy of the three main branches of the O'Donnell family in the 17th century

inquisition of 1609 taken at Lifford Bishop Montgomery set out his claims all over the county.[38] The bishop claimed lands and revenues not only from Rory O'Donnell, the earl of Tír Chonaill, but also from the earl's rivals such as Niall Garbh and Caffar Óg O'Donnell, and also from the other major landowners in Co. Donegal such as the McSweeneys, O'Gallaghers and O'Boyles. For example, there were 12 quarters of land in the barony of Kilmacrennan, which were 'litigious between the bishop of Raphoe and the late earl of Tír Chonaill'. As well as this there were 4 additional quarters of ecclesiastical land nearby from which 'O'Donnell had, time out of mind, 18 methers of butter, and 18 methers of meal, coshering'.[39] Much ecclesiastical land in Co. Donegal was held by the hereditary coarb and erenagh familes. Many of these families, such as O'Friel coarb of Kilmacrennan, paid traditional dues to the lord of Tír Chonaill or other secular lords in the county. The Coarb O'Friel paid O'Donnell from 'Kilmacrennan 24 methers … of butter, and 48 methers of meal every season. A third of a mether of mead and the mether of O'Donnell in addition to that mether'.[40] The earl of Tír Chonaill mortgaged the termon of Kilmacrennan containing '30 quarters of abbey land' in conjunction with 21 additional quarters in Cinél Móen to Alderman Nicholas Weston of Dublin for £1,600 sterling.[41] In 1609 Bishop Montgomery was attempting to get the 30 quarters at Kilmacrennan back for his diocese.

Bishop Montgomery's relentless search for land in Donegal, which he was determined to regain, created great unrest in the county among the major secular landowners. His desire to deprive 'the temporal lords of Glenfinn' of their traditional duties of 'four methers of butter and eight methers of meal coshering' from the erenagh of the parish of Donaghmore, alienated Niall Garbh O'Donnell and the O'Donnells of Castlefinn, who could have been natural allies of the new bishop against the earl of Tír Chonaill. Similarly Montgomery alienated Sir Cahir O'Donerty the lord of Inishowen, when he attempted to stop the tribute of 'four methers of butter and eight methers of meal per annum', which 'O'Doherty hath anciently had … upon every quarter of coarb land, termon land and erenagh land within the said barony of Inishowen'.[42] Montgomery even claimed land from English officers who had been given small grants by the king. However, he went too far when he attempted to recover the Island of Derry from the new town being built there and the king transferred Montgomery to the diocese of Meath in Leinster.

King James also made grants before 1610 to some English captains in Co. Donegal. In 1603–4 Captain Ralph Bingley was granted the abbey at Rathmullan in McSweeney Fanad's country, Inch Island, which was part of Sir Cahir O'Doherty's lordship, and Tory and Aran islands off the west coast which were the lands of a first cousin of the earl of Tír Chonaill, Shane McManus Óg O'Donnell.[43] Captain Bingley's brothers John and Richard also received grants of some lucrative fisheries in Co. Donegal at Donegal town, Killybegs and Ballyshannon, and of the customs of the port of Ballyshannon.[44]

Rory O'Donnell also granted away some fisheries and lands in the county at this time. In 1603–4 the earl granted 'unto Nicholas Weston and his heirs the moytie of the fishing of Lough Foyle in Tír Chonaill for 1,000 years'.[45] These grants brought a number of new English landholders into the county and also alienated many of the major nobles of Co. Donegal, such as Shane McManus Óg O'Donnell of Tory Island who joined O'Doherty's revolt in 1608, possibly because his lands had been granted to Captain Bingley.

The earl's tangled land reforms and the inquisitions of Bishop Montgomery ensured that the system of landholding in Co. Donegal by 1610 was weak and uncertain. Dublin merchants and the Protestant bishop laid claim to vast areas of the land in the county, much of which had been mortgaged by the earl from underneath his sub-chieftains. This served to alienate many of the Gaelic nobles of Co. Donegal and by the time of the earl's flight in 1607 even his mother Ineen Dubh may have been estranged due to the mortgage of her estate. This uncertainty of land tenure may help explain the future quiet attitude of the Gaelic population of Tír Chonaill to the plantation of Co. Donegal. The small estates they were to receive may have seemed to many at the time as a distinct improvement to the great uncertainty in which they held their lands under the earl. However, O'Doherty's rebellion following on so soon after the Nine Years War also ensured that Co. Donegal by 1610 was cowed and leaderless. The futility of a localized rebellion had been demonstrated to the local population and this was coupled with the demoralization of the traditional followers of the O'Donnell chieftains by the loss of the Nine Years War. Large areas of Co. Donegal in 1610 were also waste and depopulated. The county was ripe for plantation.

1. The plantation

A document entitled 'An abstract of his Majesty's title to the lands in the county of Donegal', preserved in the Carte Papers sets out the origins of King James' right to initiate the plantation in the county as the British construed it. This document begins:

> This country until the first year of his Majesty's reign was always a mere Irish country not governed by the covenants nor statute laws of the kingdom, nor subject to the ordinary justice of the justices, for the king's writ did not run there, neither before that time sheriff, governor, assize, or jail delivery, but ever governed by the O'Donnells, but the inhabitants thereof as lords or chieftains of the country who had cut and spend and bonnaghts or all other Irish exactions of all the inhabitants thereof ... The state of this country standing thus; his Majesty by his letters under the privy signet dated 4 September 1603 did signify his gracious pleasure unto the then lord deputy that Rory O'Donnell should be created earl of Tír Chonaill ...[1]

With Rory O'Donnell's flight from Donegal in September 1607 he was deemed to have forfeited his earldom to the king.[2] The revolt of Sir Cahir O'Doherty in April 1608 eliminated any plans the British administration may have had for sharing Tír Chonaill amongst the major sub-chieftains of the lordship. Surveyors were sent to west Ulster and by the end of 1608 a book had been prepared dividing up the counties of Donegal, Tyrone, Derry, Cavan, Fermanagh and Armagh into allotments for future settlement.[3]

County Donegal was divided up into a number of areas. The barony of Kilmacrennan, comprising the McSweeney lordships of Fanad and Doe, the O'Friel termon of Kilmacrennan, the O'Donnell territory of Clanelly and the largely unpopulated Glenveagh area, was reserved for English officers (servitors) and the native Gaelic Irish nobles who were to be given estates in the plantation. A 4,000 acre estate for Trinity College Dublin was also given to the university centred on the village of Kilmacrennan.[4] The territory of Cinél Móen was divided in two with the northern half, now called 'The precinct of Portlough' being reserved for Scottish settlers, and the southern half 'The precinct of Lifford', being kept for English planters. 'The precinct of Boylagh', was also allocated to the Scots. The entire O'Doherty peninsula of Inishowen was given to the lord deputy, Sir Arthur Chichester, the heart of the old lordship of the O'Donnell chieftains, now called the barony of Tirhugh was specially reserved for a royal fortress at Ballyshannon and various grants to English officers at Donegal town and other strategic sites in the barony. Trinity College Dublin also received much land in Tirhugh.

The plantation in Co. Donegal was led by the Lowland Scots, particularly Scots from the county of Ayrshire on the south-western coast of Scotland opposite Co. Antrim. In particular, two families from this county – the Montgomerys and Cunninghams – are associated with the plantation in Donegal. Bishop George Montgomery was from Braidstane in Ayrshire, his brother Hugh Montgomery, the future viscount of the Ards, being the local laird (a minor Scottish lord).[5] The Montgomerys had been prominent in north Ayrshire since the mid-14th century and the head of the family was created earl of Eglinton by the Scottish kings. The Cunningham family was also based in north Ayrshire since medieval times with the head of this family being created earl of Glencairn.[6] Far from settling in Co. Donegal and bringing peace and law and order to the Gaelic Irish, the Montgomery and Cunningham families had a long history of feuding in Ayrshire. In 1366 Sir Hugh Montgomery had been appointed Baillie of the barony of Cunningham, which as the name suggests was the patrimony of the family of that name. This led to raiding and burning of each other's castles throughout the 15th and early 16th centuries. For a while the feud died down but in 1585 a Cunningham was killed attacking a Montgomery church in retaliation for which Hugh Montgomery, the fourth earl of Eglinton was assassinated by the Cunninghams in 1586. The feud then raged throughout the late 1580s and early 1590s until King James attempted, with some success, to quell the quarrel. However, in 1606 during the sitting of the Scottish parliament at Perth, the Cunningham earl of Glencairn happened to meet some Montgomerys on the street. A vicious fight broke out which left one of the Cunninghams dead. It was not until 1609 that King James was able to settle the feud once and for all.[7] While it must be admitted that the main branch of the Cunninghams who were to be settled in Donegal – the Cunninghams of Glengarnock – were not involved in the feud, the fact that these two Ayrshire families were allocated to the same county is noteworthy.[8] The Cunninghams who were planted in Co. Donegal were led by Sir James Cunningham the laird of Glengarnock. James was married to a daughter of the earl of Glencairn and was asked to participate in the plantation at the request of the king. However, he was in a poor financial position in Scotland even before the Ulster plantation, and appears to have seen the opportunity presented by the new settlement as a chance to restore his fortunes.[9] This did not happen however and Sir James fell deeper into debt having to mortgage and sell much land in Scotland. He died in 1623.[10] Sir James was joined in Donegal by three other Cunninghams from the Glengarnock branch of the family.

However, the main Scottish noblemen to emerge from the plantation in Donegal were two important courtiers and favourites of King James himself. The first, Ludovic Stuart, the second duke of Lennox (1574–1624), was in fact a cousin of the king. He had been born in France and had had a distinguished career as a diplomat and member of the king's Scottish and English privy councils. Stuart had large estates in southern Scotland in Lothian and had links with the Montgomerys. However, he was to be an absentee planter in Donegal as from 1603 he spent most of his time at the English Court.[11] The second Scottish lord was John Murray (d. 1640), who in 1624 was created earl of Annandale. Murray was a royal official in Scotland before 1603 and received lands in Fife, Lothian and Dumfrieshire from King James. Murray too based himself at the English Court after 1603 but he continued to have many duties in Scotland. However, Murray, although he was to become by far the largest landowner in west Co. Donegal by the 1620s, was also to be largely an absentee planter.[12] Bishop Andrew Knox, appointed by King James to Raphoe in 1611, was also from the south-west of lowland Scotland, his family being originally from Renfrewshire.[13] The fact that most of the major Scottish undertakers were from the south-west of lowland Scotland no doubt greatly assisted in the creation of a sense of solidarity amongst themselves and must have assisted in helping to solve problems such as transport and the recruitment of tenants. The fact that the two most prominent Scottish planters were favourites of the king based at court in England can also only have been an advantage to all the south-west Scottish undertakers in general.[14]

When the grants were made in 1610 the duke of Lennox headed the Scottish plantation in Portlough when he was given an estate of 3,000 acres. This was by far the largest original grant in the Donegal plantation awarded to an undertaker and it must have been intended that Ludovic Stuart would be the leader of the planters in Co. Donegal. Placed around Stuart were the various Cunningham undertakers. Sir James Cunningham the laird of Glengarnock received 2,000 acres at Portlough, his son John Cunningham receiving 1,000 acres at Shane McManus Óg O'Donnell's fort at Drumboy. Sir James' uncle, also called James Cunningham, was granted 1,000 acres in western Cinél Móen at the monastery of Balleeghan, while Cuthbert Cunningham, also of the Glengarnock family was awarded 1,000 acres at the old abandoned O'Donnell castle at Cuil mic an Treoin.[15] It is noteworthy that the grants to the Cunninghams were based on the territorial divisions of the O'Donnell lordship, a deliberate decision by the planners of the plantation.

In western Tír Chonaill a new barony called Boylagh and Banagh was created encompassing the territories of the O'Boyle and McSweeney Banagh chieftains. This area was sparsely populated even under the O'Donnells. Again lowland Scottish undertakers were to the fore in the grants. Sir Robert McClelland, the laird of Bomby, the head of a family with lands in Galloway, received 2,000 acres in the Rosses. Included in Sir Robert's grants were Aran Island and nine other smaller islands off the coast. George Murray, the laird of Broughton in Wigtownshire, received 1,500 acres in Boylagh, while Patrick Vans, another landowner from Wigtownshire, also received another 1,000 acres in Boylagh. These estates were very isolated and were largely comprised of poor land. They were also sparsely settled by the Gaelic Irish, although after 1610 large numbers of the native Irish migrated to the area having been displaced by the settlers from the east and the south of the county.[16] John Murray, the future earl of Annandale, did not receive any original grant in the plantation. However, he was soon to buy all of the estates in Boylagh and Banagh that were granted to the others mentioned above as they were forfeited again to the Crown in what was a very remote and unpromising region for a plantation.

The native Gaelic Irish were granted estates in the new barony of Kilmacrennan. This meant that they had to give up their traditional lordships which had existed under the O'Donnell chieftains and uproot themselves to the west of the river Swilly. However, not all prominent Gaelic nobles still in Co. Donegal in 1610 received a grant. The O'Gallagher chieftain, most likely Brian McTurlough O'Gallagher 'of Tirhugh gentleman', who was foster father to the earl of Tír Chonaill received nothing in the plantation.[17] This was almost certainly done out of a policy to limit any residual loyalty to the exiled O'Donnells in Flanders. The most influential Gaelic nobles to receive estates in the plantation in Donegal were the four remaining sub-chieftains of the O'Donnell lordship, Donal McSweeney Fanad, Sir Mulmurry McSweeney Doe, Donough McSweeney Banagh and Turlough O'Boyle, the lord of Boylagh, each of whom received a grant of 2,000 acres.[18] Another McSweeney from Fanad, Walter McSweeney also received a substantial grant of 896 acres.[19] These were large grants by the standards of the Ulster Plantation and are comparable to anything initially granted to the Scottish and English undertakers. They may also have been larger grants than what these chieftains had held in demesne in their original lordships although these were much larger territorially than 2,000 acres. Many of the dues from non demesne areas of these lordships would have been in the form of contributions of troops and the billeting of mercenaries, tributes which were now abolished in Co. Donegal. As a result the grants of 2,000 acres may have been attractive to these chieftains. However, they did suffer a loss in prestige as their castles and monasteries were taken away from them and as they moved away from their traditional localities.

The earl's mother, Ineen Dubh McDonnell, and his granduncle, Hugh McHugh Dubh O'Donnell, also received substantial estates but only for the term of their lives. When they died their lands were to go to the English captains Sir Ralph Bingley and Sir Richard Hansard. Lady Ineen received 596 acres while Hugh McHugh Dubh was given 1,000 acres and his castle at

Ramelton.[20] Ineen Dubh had remained behind after the flight of the earls and provided information against Niall Garbh O'Donnell in 1608. Hugh McHugh Dubh O'Donnell was a great warrior and had fought hard for Red Hugh O'Donnell during the Nine Years War. He remained quiet in 1608 though, and was now retired and more interested in bardic poetry than rebellion. Nevertheless as the most influential O'Donnell noble still at large in the county he had to be placated. The remainder of the grants to the native Irish were a multitude of small grants, mostly of only 128 acres, the equivalent of one quarter of land. Some of the grantees are very obscure and hard to identify but among the most prominent were Lughaidh Ó Cléirigh, the future author of the Beatha Aodha Ruaidh Uí Dhomhnaill, and Caffar O'Donnell, the eldest son of Hugh McHugh Dubh. The O'Donnells of Portlough also received a grant of 128 acres.[21]

English army officers and some Scottish officers who had served in the English army during the Irish Wars were granted estates among the Gaelic Irish in order to keep a watchful eye on them. Patrick Crawford received 1,000 acres at Letterkenny. He appears to have been a son of Owen Crawford 'a Scottish man', who settled with his wife in Tír Chonaill under the O'Donnell chieftains. The Crawfords assisted Red Hugh O'Donnell during the Nine Years War. One of the family successfully defended Ballyshannon castle against the English in 1597.[22] Patrick's brother, David, who was the earl of Tír Chonaill's butler, participated in the flight of the earls.[23] Patrick though ended up serving in the English army and was to be rewarded for his loyalty and good fortune in 1610.[24] William Stewart, another Scottish soldier, who had fought in Ireland during the O'Doherty rebellion, was given 1,000 acres in Clanelly along the shore of Lough Swilly,[25] as was Sir Richard Hansard. Captain Basil Brooke received 1,000 acres near Lough Gartan and Glenveagh. During the first years of the plantation Doe castle came to be regarded as a very important strategic site in the north-west of the county and was initially granted to Sir Richard Bingley 'to maintain and sustain'.[26] The British administration in Ireland was determined that the fortress be well garrisoned and it was regranted in 1613 to Sir John Davies the Irish attorney general.[27] Davies in turn sold the castle to John Samford, the tenant who had been living in the castle with his wife Anne for a number of years.[28] In 1608 Lord Deputy Chichester described Doe castle as 'the strongest place absolutely both by nature and art that is in that part of the kingdom'.[29] Another English official recorded that in 1608 it 'endured 100 blows of the demi cannon'.[30]

The O'Donnells of Castlefinn received grants of 128 acres to each of Niall Garbh's brothers, Hugh Boy and Donal. This branch of the O'Donnell family had possessed 43 quarters of land in Glenfinn centred on their castle at Castlefinn. This was a very substantial estate totalling 12,900 acres of land.[31] As has previously been stated, Niall Garbh O'Donnell, the lord of Glenfinn, never took out a patent for these lands, which would have made him one of the largest landowners in the Ulster Plantation. This was because he never gave up his ambition to become lord of Tír Chonaill. However, Niall Garbh ran out of time when he became entangled in the plotting surrounding the O'Doherty revolt and in 1608 he was imprisoned in the Tower of London and was never released. Although Niall Garbh's immediate family did not receive a grant in 1610, they remained on as tenants in upper Glenfinn.

A bardic poem written to commemorate Niall Garbh's death in 1626 records in three of its stanzas how the Gaelic Irish of Co. Donegal may have felt upon losing their lands in the Ulster plantation. They observe:

> Leith Cuinn, mother of supremacy, the nurse
> of the poets' brethren, is now but a bond woman,
> But that is no humiliation without a cause.
> …
> His descendants are without a patch of ground to stand on,
> They who of old were beams of strength,
> Conn Cédchathach's race,
> Long the disgrace, they for whom
> Fiontan's soil was once fittingly bespread with colours.
> …
> Her hunting woods are streets,
> Her people are but vassals,
> Her chieftains hold not their ancestors' soil,
> The hero's wounds are the reason of it.[32]

In these stanzas the poet captures the sense of loss and degradation of status felt by the family of one prominent Gaelic noble in Tír Chonaill as they had to adjust to a new life as tenants in a settler dominated Co. Donegal. Although the poem was composed for the O'Donnells of Castlefinn, its sentiments were most likely felt by the majority of the Gaelic Irish population of the county.

The future of the lands of Tír Chonaill also weighed heavily on the minds of the exiled nobility of Donegal. The leader of the exiled O'Donnells in Spanish Flanders at this time was 'The Lady Nuala, sister to O'Donnell that died in Spain and now tutoress to the late earl of Tír Chonaill's son, living at Louvain'.[33] Nuala O'Donnell was a highly respected figure amongst the Irish exiles living on the Continent and she often spoke to Archduke Albert, the joint ruler of the Spanish Netherlands, about Irish affairs.[34] As the guardian of Rory O'Donnell's 7-year-old son Hugh Albert O'Donnell, who was recognized as the second earl of Tír Chonaill by the Spanish,[35] in early April 1614 Lady Nuala invited the British ambassador to the Spanish Netherlands, William Trumbull to her lodgings in Brussells to discuss the future of her young nephew and the earldom of Tír Chonaill. Nuala was very concerned lest word of the meeting leak out to the Spanish authorities and sent the invitation to Trumbull 'late in the evening … (as secretly as they could) to request me to come to her lodgings (not daring as they protested to come to mine)'. In a record of the encounter sent to King James himself, Ambassador Trumbull recorded that Nuala 'first began some vows and protestations of duty and observance to your Majesty and afterwards convincing me to be secret, in that she should as well'. Trumbull continues that the Lady O'Donnell offered to bring the young second earl of Tír Chonaill over to the British. Trumbull states that Nuala 'told me, she could not in any other matter do your Majesty so much service, as in the withdrawing the said young gentleman from hence, wherein she would require assistance'. According to the ambassador 'The principal point she did then urge, was your Majesty's grace and pardon for the said gentleman, together with the restoring of his father's lands'. Ambassador Trumbull told Lady O'Donnell that he had no authority to help in the proposed escape or flight of the young earl 'without your Majesty's special order', but for Nuala's 'contentment', Trumbull promised to 'acquaint your Majesty (as soon as I could) with the overture she had made unto me concerning her kinsman'. Ambassador Trumbull was as good as his word to Nuala and advised King James 'I suppose (and want not grounds for my supposition) that if it may stand with your Majesty's good liking to call home the aforesaid young gentleman'.[36] However, King James does not appear to have been very interested in Nuala O'Donnell's offer and she did not contact Ambassador Trumbull again.

Loyalty to the earl's family continued to exist in Co. Donegal, particularly amongst the earl's household families – the traditional followers of the O'Donnell chieftains. For example in 1610 David Crawford, who in 1607 had left Ireland in the ship which had carried away the earls,[37] and was described in 1610 as 'servant and butler to the late earl of Tír Chonaill', landed at Killybegs with letters from Hugh O'Neill, the exiled earl of Tyrone, to his sons-in-law. Once ashore Crawford 'lay in the house of one Owen McGettigan, in the county of Donegal, which Owen is bailiff to the sheriff there'. Owen proceeded to accompany Crawford into Monaghan and Co. Down to deliver the letters.[38] Owen McGettigan was from one of the traditional household families of the O'Donnell chieftains. Even into the 1620s old officials of Red Hugh O'Donnell were passing down traditional administrative documents from the O'Donnell lordship.[39] In 1632 an Owen McFerganan O'Gallagher: 'for high treason … was executed the last assizes for the Co. of Donegal'.[40] While it is not recorded exactly what O'Gallagher was executed for it may have been for continued opposition to the Ulster Plantation and loyalty to the exiled O'Donnell earl.

Some accounts have survived from the early years of the plantation to record how the new land owners went about organizing the settlement of their estates. In 1632, the by now elderly Bishop Andrew Knox, who was appointed Protestant bishop of Raphoe in 1611, was accused of having passed 'leases and grants to the prejudice of the church and the disabling of the succeeding bishops'. However, in his defence Bishop Knox wrote a letter detailing the measures he took to plant his ecclesiastical lands. Bishop Knox writes:

> It is not unknown (my good lords) that in time above the special commandment, of King James of blessed memory I was translated to this bishopric which I now hold, the rents therein of the same, not exceeding £30 sterling per annum. The exiguity whereof being considered by his then majesty, his royal pleasure was that annually I should have of the exchequer of England £100 sterling. This then being the sum all revenue of this bishopric being waste and without inhabitants for the most part and seeing little appearance of the increasing of the rents from the then natives and less hope of their reformation and conformity to the true religion, I resolved to return to Scotland which I did perform, and agreed with a great number of honest people, both of gentlemen and yeomen to transport themselves and families to this bishopric, to my great trouble and no small charge.

Bishop Knox continues:

> where I had brought them to the lands where they were to plant, I was constrained to give them better conditions than at first I made promise of, I report that then better conditions and better land was easy to be gotten, and therefore for their encouragement I gave to many of them the lands free from any rent for the time it pleased them, according to the years remitted in my patent, reserving upon some quarters of land more, upon lease according to the quality and good was thereof so that by the providence of God the lands belonging to this bishopric is now planted with tenants of British nation and conformable in religion to the number of 300 families and upwards, which I then and yet conceive to be a work to the glory of God and weall of the church, and to the strengthening of those parts so planted.[41]

Bringing over 300 settler families to Co. Donegal was a substantial achievement by Bishop Knox. His account also records the difficulties faced by planter landowners in the county in attracting British settlers because Donegal was at a disadvantage due to its remoteness and infertility compared to other planted counties in Ulster. By 1632 Bishop Knox states that the revenue of the bishopric of Raphoe was 'between five and £600 by the year' which was a great advance on £30 in 1611. No doubt Bishop Knox's efforts were undertaken on a greater or lesser scale by all the other undertakers in Co. Donegal, although some major landholders such as John Murray, the earl of Annandale, either did not actively recruit settlers or could not hold onto them in the remote western districts of Donegal.

The most successfully planted area in Co. Donegal was the Scottish precinct of Portlough, which became known as the Laggan during the 17th century. Phillips' and Hadsor's survey of 1622 records extensive building and Scottish settlement. The Scots built a new town for themselves, St Johnston, which had 30 buildings in 1622, some of stone, others of clay, two water mills, a tucking mill, the foundations of a church and 15 more stone houses in the surrounding area. The Cunninghams in the Laggan also built large houses, defensive bawns and settled substantial numbers of Scots, the majority of whom were armed. Sir James Cunningham of Portlough increased the size of his estate to 3,000 acres, while John Cunningham and Cuthbert Cunningham still had 1,000 acre estates in 1622. Ludovic Stuart, the duke of Lennox, assigned his 3,000 acres to Sir John Stewart who 'hath built a castle of lime and stone upon the river of Lough Foyle, 50 foot long, 25 foot broad and three storeys and a half high, slated with four flankers on the top thereof, and an iron door, portcullis wise'.[42] St Johnston was on the duke's proportion and his estate and that of one neighbour in 1622 had 134 British settlers 'whereof armed 124'.[43] Canny writes that 'the possibility of becoming involved in the plantation in Ulster aroused wide interest in land-hungry Scotland'.[44] As a result it is no surprise that the estates of the Scottish undertakers who were fortunate enough to receive good land in Co. Donegal were heavily settled.

By 1622 John Murray, who was soon to be created earl of Annandale, managed to acquire almost all of the original allocations in Boylagh and Banagh 'being eight proportions of land containing 10,000 acres'. At first Sir Robert Gordon of Lochinvar bought out the original undertakers in 1614 and 1615 with the agreement of the king due to the lack of progress in the plantation of this part of Donegal. Murray, in turn, received a grant of the entire barony from the king in 1618, again due to Gordon's lack of building and settlement on these remote and poor lands. Murray had financial assistance from Sir Archibald Atcheson, one of the secretaries of state for Scotland and a member of the Scottish privy council. A release Murray caused Atcheson to agree to in August 1632 refers to 'the occasion of all suits and controversies between him the said Sir Archibald Atcheson and the right honourable John earl of Annandale touching the great proportion of the Rosses containing by estimation 2,000 acres of land more or less and other, lands, tenements and hereditaments lying and being in the barony or precinct of Boylagh and Banagh in the county of Donegal'.[45] The same document records that Murray paid Atcheson a large sum of money 'for the appeasing of all other differences and controversies what so ever between the said Sir Archibald Atcheson and the said John earl of Annandale'. Atcheson agreed to cancel any claims he had on any of Murray's lands in the Rosses and Boylagh, which suggests that he may have been one of Murray financial backers or business partners up until

1632. There were later allegations that John Murray acquired some of his proportions by unfair means, especially in the case of the estate of his relations, the Murrays of Broughton, but other original undertakers such as Sir Robert McClelland sold up to transfer to more fertile areas in Co. Derry.[46]

The future earl of Annandale's estates had serious problems, chief of which were the poor nature of the land and an almost total absence of British settlers. A later survey of Co. Donegal recorded that on Murray's lands in the barony of Boylagh and Banagh 'the soil in general is mountain, bog and unprofitable ground, the corn being altogether poor and small, oats, some barley, but neither wheat nor rye'.[47] In 1622 the proportion of Boylagh Outragh, which was based on the O'Boyle territory of Ballyboyle and was close to Donegal town had only 27 British settlers, of which 17 were 'meanly armed'.[48] The proportion of Cargie had 32 British men settled, with 17 'reasonable well armed'. The proportion of Duncaneely, which was based on the previous McSweeney Banagh lordship, had 44 British present, with 18 'meanly armed'. Murray changed the name of McSweeney's castle at Rahin to Castle Murray, which was well fortified and the home of his agent Herbert Maxwell and his family.[49] The situation was even worse on Murray's proportions of Kilkerane, Mullaneagh, Boylagh Utragh, the Rosses and Moynargon, which lay along the isolated west coast of the county and had virtually no British settlers and no inhabited fortifications. In fact, Boylagh Utragh had only one British family settled on it and the Rosses none at all.[50] From an official British point of view this was a very unsatisfactory situation as these proportions became the heartland of the Gaelic Irish native population in Co. Donegal throughout the 17th century. An official abstract prepared for Lord Deputy Falkland written in 1623 specifically expresses concern at the situation on the earl of Annandale's estates. This report records that:

> The earl of Annandale hath near two baronies, the McSweeneys' country, and most of them continue there as tenants, a dangerous and discontented people, and full of fastnesses. It is necessary a certain number of men should be in readiness and maintained by him and his tenants for all occasions.[51]

This report acknowledges that Murray's estates were unsupervised and still in the hands of the dispossessed Gaelic Irish. In light of what was to happen in Co. Donegal in 1641 it is unknown if Murray ever acted upon these recommendations to improve security on his lands. However, it is likely that he did nothing.

Murray also controlled the port of Killybegs which is called 'the new borough town … consisting of a provost and 12 burgesses', in 1622. However, the site although described as 'one of the best harbours in this kingdom' had only 17 inhabitants, some of whom were Irish. Again in 1626 the earl of

Annandale had difficulties with the Killybegs part of his estate. A family called Neville ran the earl's fishery in the town. However, their equipment 'their nets and cordage they were not worthy of such one as the provision for such a fishing required'. James Lord Balfour who was assisting the earl with the running of Killybegs states that Annandale was 'well rid of them'. There were problems with the earl's leases in the town and the collection of his rents. Murray seems to have fallen out with his agent, Herbert Maxwell, who Balfour wrote to the earl was 'well informed with the passages of your proceedings as it will not be safe for you to distrust him till you can solidly retire him with that satisfaction as may in some sort give him content'. Sir Paul Gore was appointed to collect Annandale's rent in the town 'and to have your whole money in readiness upon eight days warning', although arrears were not forthcoming despite 'all the threatenings' Balfour could muster. Balfour commented that 'there is great hopes of fishing this year', but that it had been 'carelessly neglected'. Lord Balfour made a well-judged comment to the earl of Annandale when he also wrote 'Your own presence here could work greater effects with five days stay than your friends or servants can perform with a year's labour'.[52] It appears that the many salmon fisheries on the earl of Annadale's lands were the profitable parts of his estate and fisheries belonging to Murray are recorded on the river Eske, the Eany Water at Inver and at Teelin, which were all situated in Donegal Bay and the Owenree river in Boylagh.[53]

One can only conclude that the earl of Annandale's immense estate which stretched westward and northward from Donegal town, along the coastline of Co. Donegal, up to the border with the barony of Kilmacrennan, was a troubled and extremely lightly planted area which needed the attention of a resident lord rather than an absentee at Court. In 1629, the new king, Charles I, who may have heard rumours about Annandale's estate, ordered a commission 'to inquire whether John Murray, earl of Annandale, has broken the condition upon which he was granted certain lands in the barony and precinct of Boylagh and Banagh in Co. Donegal'.[54] However, Sir Paul Gore who collected the earl's rents was on the commission so that it is no surprise that four months later the king, upon receipt of a favourable report ordered Lord Deputy Falkland 'to pass under the great seal, a bill granting 10,000 acres in the baronies of Boylagh and Banagh in the Co. Donegal to the earl of Annandale'.[55]

In between the success of the Laggan plantation and the difficulties with the estate of the earl of Annandale lay the plantation settlements of the English at Lifford and the servitors in Tirhugh and the barony of Kilmacrennan. A small number of the English and Scottish servitors in the barony of Kilmacrennan had also made good progress, particularly along the shore of Lough Swilly. Patrick Crawford was killed in 1614 while helping to suppress a MacDonald rebellion in the Hebrides.[56] The new owner of his proportion, Sir George Merbury, built a market town at Letterkenny, which had 50 thatched houses in 1622 and 64 British male settlers, 40 of these being armed.[57]

North along the shore of Lough Swilly lay the estate of Sir William Stewart. Stewart built a bawn at Fort Stewart and an impressive castle and town at Ramelton. In 1622 Ramelton had '40 houses and cabins, thatched, inhabited by Britons', with the foundations of a church and 'a street, well paved'. The castle was 'of lime and stone, slated, 48 foot long, 23 foot broad and 34 foot high, being three storeys and half high, with three round flankers on the top of the castle, and a round turret or staircase, 42 foot high, with a battlement and platform'.[58] Stewart had 39 British settlers on his 2,000 acre estates, with 29 of these being armed. Bishop Knox also purchased land at Rathmullan on the shore of Lough Swilly and built 'a good house of lime and stone, slated, in some part three storeys and in other two storeys and ½ high'. The bishop also built a village at Rathmullan, which had 45 houses 'inhabited by Britons' in 1622.[59] The other proportions of the servitors, such as those of Thomas Dutton in Rosguill and at Doe castle were very lightly settled, with none or very few British tenants. However, Doe castle, 'an ancient strong castle, three stories high, and a bawn of lime and stone about the same 120 foot square and 16 foot high, with good flankers, standing on a good harbour, called Sheep Haven', was 'well repaired' by Captain Samford.[60]

The 1622 Survey concludes its section on Co. Donegal with the observation that 'Upon all the said proportions in the county of Donegal, the number of natives do generally far exceed the Britons'.[61] The survey also records information on the estates of the major Gaelic Irish nobles who received large grants of land in the plantation. The most successful in 1622 was Turlough O'Boyle, who had been lord of Boylagh in pre-plantation times. A slightly earlier survey taken in 1619 recorded that Turlough, along with his 'tenants and followers' had 'removed to the proportion assigned unto them'.[62] O'Boyle built a large stone house at Faugher, which he rented out to an Englishwomen, Mrs Stanton, who had four English tenants.[63] By 1641 O'Boyle had increased his land holdings to over 4,000 acres or 11 quarters of land in the parishes of Clondahorky and Raymunterdoney.[64] Turlough was one of the few Gaelic nobles in Co. Donegal who increased his estate after the plantation. Walter McSweeney also appears to have adjusted well to the plantation as he built a small castle of lime and stone and was appointed a justice of the peace.[65] The other McSweeneys who had received estates of 2,000 acres were not as successful. Donal McSweeney Fanad built 'a house of clay and stone, 36 foot long, 22 foot broad, a storey and a half high, the floor and roof of birch timber, thatched'. The survey recorded that part of McSweeney's bawn (the surrounding defensive wall) had 'fallen down'.[66] By 1622 Sir Mulmurry McSweeney Doe had fallen on hard times and his house was 'lying waste, some part of the materials being there ready to finish the same'.[67] Local tradition has it that this McSweeney chieftain 'drank out his estate, but to whom he mortgaged it is not remembered'.[68] The estate of McSweeney of Banagh is not recorded in the 1622 survey. Pynnar's survey of 1619 states that

Donough McSweeney Banagh and his followers had not made the move to their plantation estate in the barony of Kilmacrennan but had 'bought grazing of Alexander Kernes, general agent for the Scottish undertakers in the precinct of Boylagh and Banagh'.[69] Perhaps McSweeney sold his estate to Turlough O'Boyle in order to remain on his family lands in Banagh. The 1619 survey also records that the major Gaelic Irish landowners in Co. Donegal did not issue leases (estates) to their tenants, most of whom continued to farm in the traditional way, 'to plough after the Irish manner'.[70]

A number of sources, dating from the 1620s, comment on the poverty of the Gaelic Irish population of Co. Donegal after the plantation. Eoin O'Cullinane, the Catholic bishop of Raphoe, lamented the fact that there were so few natives of substance left that he was finding it difficult to maintain himself.[71] The vicar general of Raphoe, Conor O'Boyle, was fortunate enough to be sheltered by his wealthy relative Turlough O'Boyle, at his house at Kiltoorish, but by the 1630s Bishop O'Cullinane, in despair, was asking to be transferred to the richer diocese of Derry, part of which lay within Co. Donegal.[72] The 1622 survey also recorded that woodkerne were still active in Donegal where they preyed on the Gaelic Irish natives who 'go a creting and live in cabins dispersedly, being not able upon occasion to relieve one another … [and] take meat and whatsoever else they think fit from them'.[73] Strong local government was needed in the county to erase the bandit problem which had a long history in Tír Chonaill. The bandit scourge was worst in the isolated west of the county on the earl of Annandale's estates. In October 1628 it was stated that there were '16 woodkerne in one company' based in the valley of the Owenree river on the Rosses side of the Derryveagh Mountains. These woodkerne 'committed several robberies' and even attempted to attack the house of one of the settlers 'Lady Mervyn', but were beaten off.[74] Although the presence of woodkerne in the mountains throughout the 1620s made travel in parts of Co. Donegal dangerous, as long as the woodkerne confined the majority of their depredations to the Gaelic Irish of the county, their existence was, to an extent, tolerated by the British authorities.

The Gaelic culture of Co. Donegal flourished at home at this time and also among the exiles living at Louvain in Spanish Flanders. Lughaidh Ó Cléirigh wrote a biography of Red Hugh O'Donnell, the Beatha Aodha Ruaidh Uí Dhomhnaill, and participated in Iomarbhágh na bhFileadh – the Contention of the bards, a lively poetical contest between the bardic poets of Munster and Ulster which took place from 1616. The Gaelic noble Hugh McHugh Dubh O'Donnell, a learned amateur poet, also took part in the Contention.[75] The Irish College at Louvain at this time was a centre of Irish learning. One of the O'Clery's from Tirhugh, Tadhg an tSléibhe, left Donegal to become a Franciscan. He took the name Mícheál at Louvain and was sent back to Ireland in 1626 to collect ancient Gaelic manuscripts, a project Ó Cléirigh worked

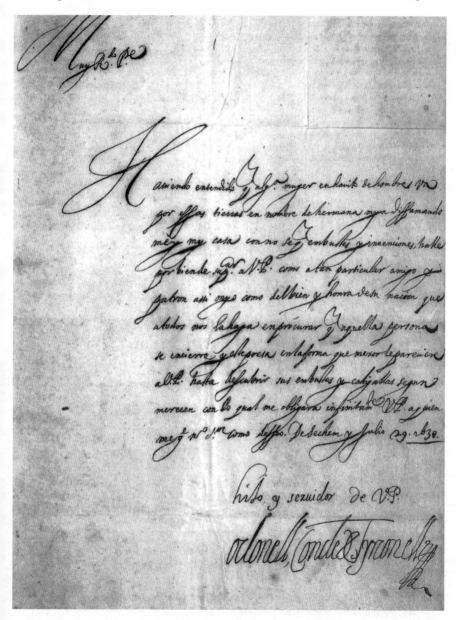

3 Spanish letter signed by the second earl of Tír Chonaill giving notice of his estrangement from his sister Maria (UCD Archives, Franciscan MS D2, f.151).

on from 1626 to 1630.[76] In early 1632 Mícheál and three companions set themselves up at the isolated house of the Donegal Franciscans at Bundrowes, on the very southern border of Co. Donegal, where they began to write the Annals of the Four Masters. They finished in 1636.[77] There were additional talented Donegal Franciscans at Louvain at this time including Mícheál Ó Cléirigh's director, Aodh Mac an Bhaird and John Colgan from Inishowen.

Nuala O'Donnell, who also lived in Louvain until her death in the early 1630s, owned a book of bardic poetry, now known as The Book of O'Donnell's Daughter, which contains many poems written for the O'Donnell chieftains.[78] A collection of bardic poetry was also written for Bishop O'Cullinane.[79] O'Cullinane spent time at Louvain where he was tutor to the young second earl of Tír Chonaill. The bishop had been brought up in the household of the O'Donnell chieftains ('Princely rearing Eoin received', as a bardic poet put it). Some bardic poetry written for Bishop Eoin records what must have been strenuous efforts he made to maintain the Catholic faith of his Gaelic Irish flock as he was:

> Everywhere baptizing crowds:
> Marvellous display of love;
> To befriend his people thus:
> Weary toil he underwent.[80]

All this activity suggests a vibrant community.

Throughout the early 1620s Niall Garbh O'Donnell continued to be imprisoned in the Tower of London. He lived in poverty in prison as his tenants had turned on his family in 1613 when they refused to pay their obligations to his wife and infant son.[81] Niall Garbh, even in prison, continued to be an important figure in Gaelic Ireland. In 1624 it was reported that 'Irishmen coming out of the Low Countries have been admitted to visit Niall Garbh in the Tower'. However, Lord Deputy Falkland got to hear of this and wrote to the English authorities that 'no good counsel can be expected from him, and therefore that liberty fit to be restrained'.[82] Niall Garbh's son Neachtan died in the Tower in 1624. Niall himself died in 1626 aged 57 'having been in the hand of King James for a long time before that'.[83] Niall's family had bardic poems commissioned upon both the death of himself and Neachtan.[84]

Rory's two children, his son Hugh Albert O'Donnell and his daughter Mary Stuart O'Donnell (she preferred to call herself Maria), continued to hold a fascination for the Gaelic Irish population of Co. Donegal. Hugh Albert grew up to become a highly respected nobleman in Spanish Flanders. In 1625 O'Donnell entered the Spanish army as a captain in the cavalry and also received a knighthood at this time. In 1632 he was promoted to colonel and given command of his own Irish regiment.[85] Around 1632, O'Donnell married

4 Letter dealing with personal matters signed by Maria Stuart O'Donnell (reproduced by permission of Biblioteca Apostolica Vaticana, all nights reserved).

Anne Margueritte, a daughter of the Count de Boussu. Illustrating the high respect the young second earl was still held in Co. Donegal, a bardic poet Fearghal Óg Mac an Bhaird composed a poem for O'Donnell, beginning 'Fogus furtacht don Tír Thuaidh'.[86] Maria Stuart O'Donnell was brought up in London under the supervision of the British authorities. However, in 1629 she escaped along with her two cousins Conn O'Donnell and Hugh O'Rourke. A set of Gaelic annals from Co. Donegal records the event. It states:

> 1629: Conn son of Caffar son of Hugh McManus, and the daughter of the earl of Tír Chonaill, and Hugh O'Rourke son of Tadhg escaped from London.[87]

Maria's escape from England created something of a sensation in Flanders.[88] Initially she got on well with her brother and the Irish exile community. However, when she refused Archbishop Conry's offer to be married to John O'Neill the third earl of Tyrone, because she loved a Donegal man, Captain Dualtagh O'Gallagher, Maria was disowned by her brother and the émigré community.[89] She left for Austria with O'Gallagher where they had a son but O'Gallagher was killed while serving in the Austrian army in the 1630s. Maria Stuart O'Donnell was last recorded living in Rome but it is not known when she died or what became of her son.[90]

From 1610 the plantation in Donegal made good progress in the east and south of the county, where there was fertile land and despite the vagaries of the weather during the first decade. (1612 was known for 'An samhradh te' – the warm summer and 1613 for 'An sneachta mór' – the big snowfall).[91] In areas where there was a large turnover in the owners of some of the planted proportions, the progress of the plantation was set back, particularly on the earl of Annandale's estate on the western seaboard. Ludovic Stuart and the Cunninghams of the Laggan were diligent and conscientious planters, whereas John Murray, the earl of Annandale, who became the planter with by far the largest estate in terms of acreage in the west of the county, was an absentee with serious problems on his estate and very few British settlers. The activities of Bishop Knox on his lands demonstrated what a determined planter could achieve, but Co. Donegal was at a definite disadvantage in relation to the other planted areas of Ulster due to its remoteness and poor quality of land. However, by 1622 the plantation had put down strong roots in the east of the county, along the shores of Lough Swilly and in the towns of south Donegal. The Gaelic Irish population still predominated in most areas of the county, with the western coastline becoming the new focus for the Gaelic natives.

2. The revolt of 1641

An abstract of a report prepared for Lord Deputy Falkland in 1623 recorded that the province of Ulster:

> had formerly been the most potent and turbulent province. The six escheated counties coming to the crown, by Tyrone's revolt and running away are so weakly planted by the undertakers, as without speedy proceeding, upon any stir of the Irish, they will be supplanted.[1]

Certainly there were many problems with the Ulster plantation, not least in Co. Donegal and the authorities were feeling vulnerable. As has been stated in the previous chapter, although the plantation in Co. Donegal had made substantial progress in the Laggan and in the towns in the south of the county, other areas, particularly in the west, were very lightly settled. The same report stated that at present the province was quiet due to the 'want of the native power'. However, the Gaelic Irish were 'discontent' due to their aversion to British government, the established religion and their recent dispossession from 'the lands they formerly held'. It was also stated that the continued depredations of the English garrisons and 'the persuasion of their priests' continued to unsettle the population. In particular Lord Deputy Falkland feared 'the encouragement of pretenders unto titles of great territories to seek aid abroad and stir up their late followers at home, namely Tyrone's son, claiming the county of Tyrone [and] a good part of Armagh, Tír Chonaill's son, claiming the territories of Tír Chonaill and Donegal etc., and young O'Cahan, pretending the part of the county of Coleraine'.[2] The English administration in Ireland had good reason to fear for the future of the Ulster plantation in the 1620s and 30s. The exiled archbishop of Tuam, Florence Conry, based at the Irish College of Louvain in Flanders, was a dangerous and unceasing opponent of the plantation. In 1627, one year after war broke out between Britain and Spain, Conry submitted a plan to King Philip IV for the Irish regiment in Flanders to land at and fortify Killybegs, and capture Derry city. Hugh Albert O'Donnell, the second earl of Tír Chonaill and John O'Neill, the third earl of Tyrone were to be the leaders of the proposed expedition, which was to set up an Irish parliament in Derry once support from other Irish lords was received, and then seek recognition from foreign powers.[3] However, nothing developed from this plan and Conry died in 1629.

In March and April 1627 Lord Deputy Falkland received information linking Bishop Eoin O'Cullinane and other members of his family, at home in Donegal and on the Continent, to the conspiracy. It was stated that the bishop was at 'the court in Spain soliciting an invasion by the Irish regiments in the Low Countries'. The bishop's brother Brian, a Cistercian abbot living in Flanders was also stated to be involved as was their cousin Glasny O'Cullinane, who was said to 'lie in Tirhugh to prepare the people'.[4] Bishop O'Cullinane was accused of importing 'two barrels of books landed at Drogheda'. It was alleged that these books contained seditious propaganda in favour of John O'Neill, the third earl of Tyrone, being 'A declaration of Tyrone's title to Ulster, with a signification to all people in Ireland, that the king of Spain was resolved to send him over with an army in July next, and in Ulster to denounce him king thereof, and there to crown him, and that with all he should be governor of all Ireland in the king of Spain's behalf'. However, these accusations were greatly exaggerated and unfounded. There was only one informant, a disgruntled priest, 'but one witness … a priest as well himself', as Lord Deputy Falkland put it. Although Glasny O'Cullinane was arrested in March 1627 and brought to Dublin castle, Falkland himself doubted 'whether he should rack the traitor', as the information given against O'Cullinane was weak and 'many' in Co. Donegal were 'startled at this man's apprehension'.[5] Bishop O'Cullinane, upon his return to Raphoe, was also arrested by the British authorities in 1628, but later released.[6] The Bishop certainly had links with the exiled second earl of Tír Chonaill and the O'Cullinanes had been a favoured household family who had loyally served the pre-plantation O'Donnell chieftains. The barrels of books imported into Drogheda most likely contained religious material for use in the diocese of Raphoe and the entire episode may owe more to religious persecution than a plot by the O'Cullinane family to overthrow the plantation of Ulster.[7]

Turlough O'Boyle, by far the most substantial Gaelic Irish landowner in Co. Donegal at this time, was also arrested in 1628 as part of the scare. O'Boyle was accused of receiving letters and many visitors, who had travelled from Spain, at his house at Kiltooris, including Neachtan O'Donnell, a relative of the first earl of Tír Chonaill. Neachtan had participated in the flight of the earls in 1607 and had been serving ever since in the Spanish army in Flanders.[8] O'Boyle certainly received news of the plans of the exiled earls as it was common knowledge 'amongst the servants of the house that the Spaniards would come into this kingdom before it were long … and the Killybegs the place of their landing'. Very serious allegations were made against Turlough, by his butler, Edmond O'Grady, who alleged that: 'all the young men about his master's habitation, as many as he doth trust, were all combined and resolved to join with the Irish regiments and Spaniards if they came; and that there was not a boy belonging to his master or his friends, but were all armed with *scians* and darts at the least, and others better'.[9] Although these accusations may indicate one of the first organized attempts by the Gaelic natives to attack the Ulster plantation, they are probably not credible. Lord Deputy Falkland took an interest in the goings on in Boylagh and had Sir William Stewart arrest O'Boyle and Neachtan O'Donnell. After initial confinement in Stewart's house, O'Boyle was 'sent ... to the jail of the Lifford there to remain till he be delivered by true course of law or until your lordship [Lord Deputy Falkland] signify your further pleasure'. Neachtan O'Donnell was 'also in the jail of Lifford', and Stewart advised Lord Deputy Falkland to 'send for him, for I believe he hath something in his mind, that he may be made to discover'. However, O'Donnell would 'confess nothing' to Stewart.[10] If Turlough O'Boyle had indeed been plotting an attack on the settlers in Donegal he would surely have been executed as were a group of unfortunate Gaelic nobles in Co. Derry in 1615.[11] In the end O'Boyle was simply released.

Certainly in the 1630s the settlers still feared for their security. From 1636–7 the Protestant bishop of Raphoe, John Leslie, built a fortified palace which cost him £3,500.[12] By this time there were many hundreds of settlers planted in the barony of Raphoe and in the south of the county stretching from Ballyshannon in Tirhugh along the coast to Killybegs. However, the mountainous interior of the county and the remote west had very few settlers and remained overwhelmingly Gaelic Irish in population.[13] The older generation of Gaelic nobles who had accepted the plantation was also passing away. Donal McSweeney Fanad died c.1622; his son Donal Gorm died on 17 February 1637.[14] Sir Mulmurry McSweeney Doe died in the 1630s, as did Donough McSweeney Banagh.[15] Some of their successors had not known warfare in Ireland and were to prove to be open to the counsel of dangerous and more desperate men.

The origins of the revolt which broke out in mid-Ulster on 22 October 1641 are complex. The prime instigators were Gaelic Irish nobles who had done well out of their fathers' loyalty to the English crown during the Nine Years War, but who had fallen on hard times. There were thousands of troops demobilized from Lord Deputy Wentworth's army at large about the country. Trouble was brewing in Scotland with the covenanters and with the parliament in England. For the purposes of this study the prime origin was the conspiracy hatched in mid-Co. Tyrone by Sir Phelim O'Neill, the lord of Kinard. Sir Phelim was in contact by means of a cipher 'a table with a character' with Colonel Owen Roe O'Neill, a nephew of Hugh O'Neill (d. 1616), the second earl of Tyrone, who commanded his own Irish regiment in Flanders.[16] Colonel O'Neill had grown up in Ulster and was eager to return as he appears to have grown tired of service in the Spanish army in Flanders and felt he could do well in the opportunities presented by any new war in Ireland.

It is not clear how closely involved the Gaelic Irish exiles from Co. Donegal were in the plotting of the rising. On the Continent, the earls of Tyrone and Tír Chonaill detested each other and were unlikely to communicate. In 1642

Mícheál Ó Cléirigh writing in Flanders recorded of Colonel Hugh Albert O'Donnell:

> In the month of October [1641] … the old Gaels and old English of Erin, for the most part, began to rise up in war against the heretics, to free themselves from every oppression that was upon them. When the Earl O'Donnell, whom we have mentioned heard of the breaking out of the war, he went in the presence of the king of Spain, and boasted of his own service, and of the death of O'Neill previously to him [John O'Neill, the third earl of Tyrone had been killed at the battle of Montjuich, near Barcelona fighting the Catalan rebels in December 1641], and all the obligations that the Spaniards were under of aiding the Irish, and he therefore requested of him to give him aid, or if not, to permit him to go home to his native country.[17]

Ó Cléirigh's note suggests that Earl Hugh Albert did not have prior knowledge of the planning of the 1641 revolt and only attempted to return to Ireland in early 1642. Far from reinforcing the Gaelic rebels in Co. Donegal, Hugh Albert O'Donnell's regiment had been in Spain since 1638, and was in Catalonia helping to suppress the Catalan revolt which had broken out in 1640.[18] An elite force, O'Donnell's regiment was needed in Spain and indeed it had already distinguished itself at the battle of Fuenterrabía fought in the Basque Country against the French in 1638. O'Donnell and his men were also present at Mountjuich in 1641 when John O'Neill was killed. However, on the retreat from Barcelona O'Donnell's men ransacked the small town of Reus 'carrying off 800 bags of plunder'.[19] To make amends to the Spanish authorities Hugh Albert and his regiment were loaded onto Spanish ships for an intended raid on the south of France. They were ambushed by the French navy on their return and O'Donnell and many of his soldiers were killed.[20] Mícheál Ó Cléirigh recorded the death of the earl in an annalistic note writing:

> The age of Christ 1642: O'Donnell who was usually called earl of Tír Chonaill; i.e. Hugh, son of Rory, son of Hugh, son of Manus, was drowned in the summer of this year in the sea which is called Mediterranean, in assisting the king of Spain in the war which broke out between him and the king of France.[21]

Whether Hugh Albert O'Donnell made any serious effort to return to Ireland is unclear. He certainly asked for the king of Spain's permission to return to Ireland, but his reaction on being refused is not recorded. If Hugh Albert had returned to Co. Donegal he could have provided much-needed leadership and invaluable military knowledge to the Gaelic Irish of Co. Donegal, just as

Colonel Owen Roe O'Neill was to provide for the Irish of the entire province after his arrival in Ulster in 1642.

It is also not very clear how closely the Gaelic Irish in Co. Donegal were involved in the plotting of the rising. Their estates in the barony of Kilmacrennan were isolated from the rest of Gaelic Ulster and there appears to have been a great deal of uncertainty about joining the rebellion. The main historical sources for the outbreak of the 1641 rebellion in Co. Donegal are Everden McSweeney's letter to Dublin dated 27 October 1641, preserved in the Irish State Papers, and the 1641 depositions 'concerning murder and robberies committed in the County of Donegal', preserved in Trinity College Dublin. Everden McSweeney was a son of Walter McSweeney and was a JP in the barony of Kilmacrennan. His letter must be used with care because, although he was a local JP and by the end of October 1641 was still attempting to be loyal to the government, one of the depositions refers to him as 'a cunning and dangerous rebel', with 'diverse bloody murders committed by his kernes and soldiers'.[22] The 1641 depositions must also be used with care, but they do preserve some accurate information.

According to Everden McSweeney events began in Co. Donegal in early October 1641. McSweeney records that there was an O'Gallagher soldier 'that newly this last summer went overseas to the Low Countries and returned from thence some three weeks past', who, when he landed back 'came with great expedition unto the friars of Donegal and presently immediately Christopher McNulty friar posted away to Galway and Sir Niall Garbh's his son to go over seas'.[23] It is unclear whether O'Gallagher was going about Co. Donegal spreading messages to the Gaelic nobles of the county from the Irish leaders in Flanders urging them to rise up in rebellion. Everden McSweeney certainly felt that the Franciscans who were based in 1641 in the remote pass of Bearnas Mór were involved. McSweeney wrote that 'if there be any draught of foreigners to aid these malicious traitors, that the Franciscan friars of Bearnas Mór doth well know of it', particularly friar McNulty whom McSweeney calls 'the greatest politician and traveller in Ireland of a friar', who McSweeney was 'fain endeavouring to get hold of'. McSweeney also relates that the rebels made O'Gallagher a captain of their forces. Everden McSweeney states that when the rebellion broke out in Co. Tyrone a second Franciscan friar Fergal Óg McWard 'gave an order in the name of Tibbot Taaffe and Sir James Dillon, unto Turlough McCaffar O'Donnell and to Turlough Óg McRory O'Donnell to gather soldiers, with Turlough McRory with his men is now in rebellion, for Turlough McCaffar I am not certain of his being with them yet'. McSweeney hints that Turlough McCaffar O'Donnell (a grandson of Hugh McHugh Dubh O'Donnell), had links with Sir Phelim O'Neill, stating that Turlough 'who brought a great many men out of these parts, is now with the O'Neills that committed the reported mischiefs '. The depositions of Ann

Dutton, from Drum near Doe castle, and John Ravenscourt from Lifford, also record Turlough McCaffar O'Donnell as being 'a captain' of the rebels.[24]

The 1641 depositions indicate that attacks on settlers in the barony of Kilmacrennan began on 31 October, over a week after the outbreak of the rebellion in Tyrone, but that some settlers were not attacked until December 1641.[25] The group of depositions made by settlers near Doe castle record the main rebel leader as being Mulmurry McSweeney 'who is grandchild to Sir Mulmurry McSweeney', the grandfather being one of the Irish natives granted a large estate in the plantation.[26] Mulrony Carroll, who made the deposition, states that the settlers were attacked on the last day of October. Mulmurry McSweeney was assisted by various other McSweeneys and men from the McFadden and O'Murray families. Two depositions record that the rebels killed the local Protestant minister, Robert Atkins: 'because he would not confess more money than he had',[27] even though one settler stated that Atkins 'had often relieved and kindly entertained them in his house'.[28] These two depositions also record that Atkins' two brothers John and Mark were 'murdered in their own barn at Clondavaddog'. There also appears to have been another atrocity near Doe castle, when the settler John McKenny, his wife and mother-in-law, were killed by James McGilbride 'a notorious rebel'. McGilbride was reported to have 'ripped up' Mrs McKenny's belly 'she being great with child'.[29] A garbled account of these killings was given by Mulrony Carroll who stated that a different set of rebels murdered three women 'one of whose bellies they ripped up, she being great with child, so as the child sprang out of her belly'.[30] Carroll refers to the McSweeneys of Doe and their followers as 'those septs being the most cruel and bloody minded people of any sept in that county of Donegal'.

The accounts of Everden McSweeney and the depositions also contain information for other parts of Co. Donegal. McSweeney records that by the end of October 1641 'I hear Turlough Óg McRory O'Donnell, Manus McÉigneachán O'Donnell and some of the Gallaghers hath raised great store of men already in Glenfinn'.[31] The deponent James Kennedy of Donegal recounted that his own servants 'robbed and despoiled him' and 'carried some of this deponent's cattle, horses and household goods to the rebel Manus O'Donnell (whose father Colonel [Niall] Garbh O'Donnell died in the Tower)'.[32] Manus O'Donnell was also based in Glenfinn. Kennedy recorded that 'his young cattle were carried away by the sept of the O'Gallaghers'. Kennedy names the leaders of the O'Gallghers as being Captain Hugh O'Gallagher, and James, Owen and Hugh Boy, the sons of Toole McCahir O'Gallagher. This deponent also recorded a third atrocity in Donegal when 'the sept of the O'Gallaghers … murdered one John Park and one Richard Gibson, John Gibson his son and David Farrell … by mangling and cutting them in pieces, whose mangled corpses this deponent saw and caused to be buried'. James Kennedy linked Turlough O'Boyle and his brother Tadhg to the outbreak of the rebellion in Co. Donegal, Kennedy stating that the O'Boyles were aware of Sir Phelim O'Neill's strategy of claiming to have a commission from King Charles I for his actions. Tadhg O'Boyle was soon captured and imprisoned in Donegal castle.

All the settlers who made depositions were plundered of their farm stock and household goods. Mulrony Carroll stated that he was 'deprived robbed and despoiled of his estate goods and chattels consisting of cattle, sheep, corn, debts, benefit of leases, money, hogs, household goods, boats, fishings and other things amounting in all to the value or same of £1,500 sterling'.[33] James Kennedy was 'deprived and robbed or otherwise despoiled of his mean goods and chattels consisting of rents, benefits and profits of his farms and free school means, and of cattle, horses, corn, hay, household stuff, debts, provision in plenty of husbandry and other goods and chattels and hath suffered spoiling of his housing whereby he hath lost for the present £600 sterling'.[34] Ann Dutton put her losses at £300, which included the loss of Drum house in the parish of Mevagh, 'a fair mansion house, which the rebels burned', destruction in this instance which is recorded in another source.[35]

One deposition from Co. Donegal, that of Christopher Parmenter of Kilmurray, appears to be a measured and an accurate account. Christopher states that 'the next day after the rebellion brake out [23 October 1641], he this deponent with his wife and family (for safety of their lives), fled from their house at Kilmurray aforesaid to Wilson's Fort in the same county where they continued until May last 1643'.[36] Parmenter records that his neighbour 'one Robert Kilpatrick and his family (Protestants that stayed behind [to the number] of six or seven), were murdered by the rebels'. However, Parmenter continues 'And this deponent hath heard of diverse other murders and cruelties in the country thereabouts but saw none, neither did he see any other extreme outrage (though he is persuaded and hath heard there were many)'. During his 18-month-stay at the Wilson's Fort refuge, the only violence Parmenter was a personal witness to was an incident 'when some of the rebels near Wilson's Fort seized on and took a poor smith that had made and headed pikes for the English, whose hands therefore they cut off and gave him a cruel wound in the face'. This measured and careful deposition contrasts with that of John Ravenscourt of Lifford who stated that 'four baronies in the said county (wherein many English and Scottish were planted) are all wasted and spoiled and a great number of the English and Scots there slain by the rebels and some escaped by flight'.[37] Some fragments from the Trinity College Depositions may be accurate in recording some of the justifications uttered by the Donegal rebels. One fragment records that 'they (meaning the rebels) now expected the fulfilling of Columcille's prophecy, which (as they did construe it) was that the Irish should conquer Ireland again'.[38] Other rebels who burned down '13 good English houses' at the Dutton settlement at Drum, 'ploughed up and sowed the very house sides, upon their express confidence declared that no more English should dwell there'.[39]

From the surviving evidence it is possible to piece together the leadership of the Gaelic Irish of Co. Donegal in the rebellion of 1641. The most prominent rebel was Manus O'Donnell of Glenfinn, the son of Niall Garbh O'Donnell. He was assisted by the O'Gallaghers and also by his elderly uncle Hugh Boy O'Donnell. In the barony of Kilmacrennan the leaders of the rebels were Mulmurry McSweeney of Doe and a group of prominent O'Donnell nobles, Turlough and Neachtan, two grandsons of Hugh McHugh Dubh O'Donnell, Manus son of Éigneachán O'Donnell, a great-grandson of Hugh McHugh Dubh and Turlough Óg son of Rory O'Donnell who was the leader of the descendants of the O'Donnells of Portlough, a noble O'Donnell family who had ruled Tír Chonaill in the 15th century.[40] All of these nobles had substantial grievances with the Ulster plantation in Co. Donegal their families having been deprived of much land and they themselves most likely having fallen on hard times by 1641.

In east Co. Tyrone Sir Phelim O'Neill and his adherents seized all the important government and settler fortifications, some on the first night, but all within the next few days. The settlers of eastern Tyrone were taken completely by surprise. William Montgomery who was in Newtownstewart in western Tyrone in October 1641 recorded his shock and that of his grandfather, Sir William Stewart, when 'a man half stripped came with a letter signifying the insurrections, murders, and burnings on all sides, committed by the Irish'.[41] Audley Mervyn, a prominent Donegal settler from the south of the county also recorded how plantation farms and villages 'proclaimed their situation afar off by their fire and smoke'.[42] Montgomery's record is important as it indicates that the settlers of Newtownstewart had warning of the Ulster uprising before they themselves were attacked. This was to be crucial to the subsequent failure of the rising of the Gaelic Irish in Co. Donegal. The settlers in west Co. Tyrone were quickly organized by their leaders, Sir William and Sir Robert Stewart. Although confusion exists as to whether Sir Robert was Sir William's brother, or alternatively a younger son of the earl of Orkney and distant relation to King James I, he was a veteran of the mercenary wars on the Continent his having served in the Scots regiments in the Swedish army from the 1610s to the 1630s.[43] Stewart's military expertise was to be of great importance. The space given to the west Co. Tyrone settlers and the hesitation of the Gaelic Irish of Co. Donegal allowed the Stewarts to gather large numbers of recruits. The Stewarts secured control of the city of Derry, a walled town and well fortified. They also quickly set about raising a regiment of infantry each of over 1,000 men comprised of settlers from eastern Donegal and western Tyrone.

The time given by the hesitation of the Irish of Co. Donegal also allowed the settlers in the south of the county to take control of the towns of Ballyshannon, Donegal and Killybegs. The settlers in the south were first organized by Sir Ralph Gore and Audley Mervyn.[44] In November 1641 Ralph Gore received a commission from King Charles I 'to raise a regiment of 500 men to oppose the rebels in Ireland', with Audley Mervyn as his lieutenant colonel.[45] As a result, when the Gaelic nobles of Donegal finally decided to join the rebels it was too late. An attack on Ballyshannon led by a Mr Nugent and Captain O'Gallagher was beaten off by Ralph Gore.[46] When the Irish returned a fortnight later led by Turlough McCaffar O'Donnell and Manus O'Donnell, who had taken over the leadership of the Co. Donegal rebels, they were again repulsed. Around the same time, Andrew Knox, a son of the late bishop beat off an attack by the O'Boyles and McSweeneys on Killybegs where 'the best McSweeney was killed'.[47]

In the barony of Kilmacrennan companies of Scottish settlers were active led by Captains James and John Cunningham and Captain John Stewart.[48] In all, the settlers in the north-west raised four large regiments, which dominated Co. Donegal and came to be called the Laggan army.[49] Much better armed than the Gaelic Irish and led by an officer with valuable military experience, the Laggan army soon took the offensive in Donegal. The barony of Raphoe was secured and raids were launched into the barony of Kilmacrennan and the west of the county. It is recorded that Sir William Stewart was 'busy in the barony of Kilmacrennan firing and burning' and many of the Gaelic Irish were killed and thousands of cattle were captured.[50] Strong folklore traditions from the Rosses in west Co. Donegal record that the islands off the western coast became places of refuge for the local inhabitants.[51] The same folklore accounts record a massacre on Aran Island where a settler raiding party cornered the inhabitants of the island in a sea cave and killed the women and children as the men fought their way out and escaped.[52]

The settlers in south Donegal decided to convey the bulk of their families and the refugees that had sought shelter in their towns north to Derry city where they could be shipped to the safety of Scotland. An attempt made by a large Irish force to ambush the convoy in the Bearnas Mór Pass was beaten off. Sir Ralph Gore was severely wounded in this engagement and died soon after.[53] The settlers concentrated their forces in the Laggan and decided to hold only the town of Ballyshannon, Donegal castle and Castle Murray in the south of the county.[54] At the same time Sir Phelim O'Neill, the leader of the Tyrone rebels attempted to relieve the settler pressure on the Donegal Irish. Friar O'Mallon's journal records that in June 1642 'The General marched on the Scots of Tír Chonaill'.[55] Sir Phelim also hoped to encourage the Gaelic Irish of the Inishowen peninsula to join the rebellion, as they had remained quiet up until then.[56] (The Gaelic Irish inhabitants of Inishowen remained peaceful throughout the war). When O'Neill encountered Sir Robert Stewart and 2,000 musketeers in the Laggan, he was forced to encamp for the night. Stewart's men gave battle to the Irish army the next day from a constructed breastwork at a place called Glenmacquin. O'Neill's forces were routed with heavy casualties.[57]

The revolt of the Donegal Gaelic Irish was a disaster. They were defeated again and again by the settlers and the attempt by the Irish in Tyrone to assist them also failed. A contemporary Irish source, the 'Aphorismical discovery of treasonable faction', states that at this time in Gaelic Ulster 'thousands of the poor Irish starved in woods, bogs, dens, and caves'.[58] The Gaelic nobles of the province were about to give up and scatter to the rest of Ireland when Colonel Owen Roe O'Neill landed from a ship at Doe castle in the west of Donegal in July 1642.[59] He had with him arms and supplies and Irish officers from the Irish regiments in Flanders and he saved the rebellion in the north of Ireland with his arrival. Colonel O'Neill sent letters to the Gaelic leaders and thousands joined him at Doe castle. Owen Roe then marched into the centre of the province. In August 1642 at a general assembly of the Gaelic nobles of Ulster Owen Roe was selected general of the Ulster army and immediately began recruiting and organizing and instilling some discipline. Sir Phelim O'Neill was demoted to president of the province.

Each county in Ulster formed its own regiment for the Ulster Gaelic army and the Donegal tercio became known as the Tír Chonaill regiment. It comprised about 1,000 men and was commanded by Manus O'Donnell, who was appointed colonel. Manus was possibly assisted by his elderly uncle, Hugh Boy O'Donnell. Hugh Boy had fought in the Nine Years War but Manus had no military experience. This was probably true of the vast majority of the new regiment. No doubt General O'Neill appointed some veterans from the Irish regiments in Flanders to train the Donegal men. Some of these may have been Donegal natives themselves. Refugee civilians from Donegal with their creaghts [caéraigeacht – cattle herds and their attendants] also attached themselves to the Tír Chonaill regiment and began to follow the Ulster army on its campaigns. This was a spontaneous development and arose by the natural desire of refugees from all over the province to seek protection from the settler armies. It also proved to be advantageous for the Ulster army as the cattle herds were able to keep General O'Neill's regiments supplied with food. Some of the Gaelic inhabitants of Donegal remained in the county by hiding in the central mountains and on the offshore islands. They led a hunted existence as they continued to be pursued by the forces of the Laggan army. The situation must have been very bad; in 1643 Eoin O'Cullinane, the Catholic bishop of Raphoe, surrendered 'on promise of quarter' to some of Sir William Stewart's men. He was imprisoned in the dungeon of Derry city jail.[60]

Bishop O'Cullinane later recorded the hatred felt by the Protestant soldiers towards the Gaelic Irish of Donegal, which was very evident when he was first captured. In an account written after the bishop had fled to the Spanish

Netherlands sometime around 1653, O'Cullinane recounted how: 'he was in such cruel manner abused by them that he was left as a man dead without life or spirit. After the expiration of two days they led him unto the bank of a great river, expostulating with him whether he had rather die by water or be executed by the sword. He replied that it was his desire rather to be put to the sword than to be drowned'. The settler soldiers proceeded to strip Bishop O'Cullinane 'wholly naked ... intending out of hand to shoot him with their muskets'. When the matches and gunpowder failed to light 'they called for their pikemen to exercise their malicious cruelty on him'. Bishop O'Cullinane was only saved when Colonel Sir James Askin arrived on the scene, and proceeded to abuse the soldiers 'with very harsh language, styling them villains and traitors that they did nothing but murder a gentleman to whom they had already given quarter'. The bishop was 'led from thence to a most horrid dungeon ... for the space of four years, during which time he never was suffered to leave the prison but once, when commanded to appear as a malefactor before their council'.[61]

In June 1643 the Laggan army commanded by Sir Robert Stewart surprised and routed part of General O'Neill's army at the battle of Clones in Co. Monaghan. General O'Neill and his son Henry barely escaped with their lives. The general's nephew, Captain Hugh Dubh O'Neill, another veteran from the Spanish army was captured and imprisoned by the Stewarts in Derry. It was said by the Gaelic Irish after this battle that: 'The Irish lost this day of gentlemen of quality and old commanders, hard upon seven score and odd men, that it was thought that Ulster would never recover the loss of that day'.[62] The Laggan army was fortunate that it had an experienced and competent commander who was regarded by his officers as 'prudent and wary'.[63] When a truce was agreed in September 1643 between the Confederate Catholic government at Kilkenny and the king's Royalist government in Dublin, the settlers in Donegal continued fighting. There were many reasons for this. The Scots in the Laggan army supported the covenanter administration in Scotland. Also, the Laggan army relied on military supplies sent to Derry by the parliament in England, although the forces of parliament were engaged in a civil war with King Charles I. In 1643 the London parliament ordered £600 be paid 'for clothes etc. for Colonel Audley Mervyn's regiment of foot', with parliament in the same year ordering a further £200 'for the freight of the ship Paul to carry clothes, victuals etc. from London to Donegal'.[64] This support kept the Laggan army fighting and aligned with the forces opposed to the king for the time being.

As regards the Gaelic Irish of Donegal, as the war progressed the prominent landowner Turlough O'Boyle became a Confederate politician representing Ulster in the Confederate Catholic general assembly.[65] In June 1646 the Tír Chonaill regiment played an important part in Owen Roe O'Neill's victory at Benburb over the Scottish army of Major General Robert Munro, a major success for the Gaelic Ulster army. However, Colonel Manus O'Donnell, the commander of the Tír Chonaill regiment was the most prominent Irish casualty on the day. An annalistic note in a small set of Donegal annals records this event and O'Donnell's subsequent funeral and burial at Armagh. It states:

> 1646: Manus son of Niall Garbh son of Conn son of the Calvagh O'Donnell was killed in the overthrow of Benburb, in Tyrone, and the falling of that person there was a source of sorrow and sadness. And especially to O'Donnells because he was the only hope of support defence and upkeep and his burial was among a great assembly of the nobles and high gentlemen of the province of Ulster in Armagh far from his native area.[66]

Manus O'Donnell's death in the battle of Benburb following four years after the death of Hugh Albert O'Donnell, the second earl of Tír Chonaill, was indeed 'a source of sorrow and sadness' to the Gaelic Irish of Co. Donegal. The next most powerful O'Donnell noble, and the only one of any substance, was now also dead. Indeed, Colonel Manus was a first cousin of Hugh Albert as his mother Nuala O'Donnell was a sister of Red Hugh and Rory O'Donnell. In the aftermath of the Confederate victory at Benburb however, many of the prominent Gaelic Irish captives held in the prison in Derry were released. Among those set free was the bishop of Raphoe, Eoin O'Cullinane.[67]

Contemporary records indicate that a Hugh Boy O'Donnell took over leadership of the Tír Chonaill regiment upon Manus O'Donnell's death. This is unlikely to have been Manus' uncle who was most likely dead by 1646 and even if he were still alive would have been extremely elderly and unfit to command. Evidence from bardic poetry indicates that the Hugh Boy O'Donnell in question was actually the son of Turlough McCaffar O'Donnell. In any event, this Hugh Boy fell out with General O'Neill over a truce with the Royalists in 1648, which split the Confederate Catholics and led to civil war. The officers of the Tír Chonaill regiment who held land in 1641 were now fearful for their estates. An anonymous source writing in 1648 from within the part of the Ulster army which hoped to reach an accommodation with the Royalists, stated of the Donegal leaders that 'John McHugh Boy O'Donnell, Turlough O'Donnell, Mulmurry McSweeney and Everden McSweeney may have or be put in a way to get and enjoy, like knights and squires, estates in the county of Donegal'.[68] With the split in the Confederate Catholics, Turlough O'Boyle, the largest Gaelic landowner in Co. Donegal in 1641, sided with General O'Neill. O'Boyle became an important supporter of O'Neill and represented the general in negotiations with the Royalists.[69] By February 1649 Hugh Boy O'Donnell had 1,200 men under his command but was ordered by the Confederate authorities to disband half of them. The remainder were dispersed into billets all over Confederate Leinster, Munster and Connacht, which in effect meant the end of the Tír Chonaill regiment.[70] According to the bardic poem beginning 'Neart gach tíre ar Thír Chonaill – The power of every country over Tír Chonaill', by the poet Somhairle Mac an Bhaird, Hugh Boy son of Turlough McCaffar O'Donnell was killed in October 1649 along with the remnants of the Tír Chonaill regiment in the massacre at Wexford when Cromwell's army stormed that town.[71]

As shown by Kevin McKenny in *The Laggan army in Ireland, 1640–1685*, the settlers in the Laggan army also began to split apart in 1648–9.[72] In late 1648 Sir Charles Coote, the new Parliamentary commander of Derry city, arrested Sir Robert Stewart as he attended a baptism in the town. Stewart was a known Royalist and was sent to be imprisoned in London.[73] In February 1649 the Ulster Scots Presbytery declared against Parliament after King Charles I was executed and 'upon this a general revolt of all the Scotch of all sides' broke out in Ulster.[74] The Scots in the Laggan army mounted a close siege of Derry city; although Sir Robert Stewart escaped from prison and returned to Ulster, Sir Charles Coote continually bested the besiegers. On 23 April 1649 Coote's forces surprised the Scots leadership at the village of Carrigans. Sixteen of the Laggan Scots were killed and 45 taken prisoner.[75] In August 1649 the villages of Carrigans and Newtown Cunningham and the small town of St Johnston were burnt down by the Derry garrison.[76] Eventually the siege was raised when General Owen Roe O'Neill's army arrived in the vicinity due to an agreement to assist Coote. In the end, the Scots in the Laggan army just went home.

Some of the Gaelic Irish of Donegal succeeded in joining the Royalists at this time. The prominent 1641 rebel leader Mulmurry McSweeney managed to convert his following into a regiment of infantry to serve the new king, Charles II. In December 1649 McSweeney received a commission as a colonel from the marquis of Ormond, the lord lieutenant of Ireland, 'to hold and maintain the garrison of the island of Tory and the rest of the islands towards and about Killybegs'.[77] In the early summer of 1650 the Ulster army appeared on the borders of the county. General O'Neill had died in November 1649 and at the Belturbet Council in March 1650 the Gaelic nobility of Ulster chose Heber McMahon, the bishop of Clogher, as his successor.[78] Despite the fact that Bishop McMahon issued a proclamation in May 1650 stating that: 'we shall make no distinction or difference between ourselves and so many of the Scottish or other nation whatsoever that now shall (as we invite them) with heart and join in his Majesty's service, or any way freely contribute to or countenance the same', when the Gaelic army arrived in Co. Donegal in June, the settlers in the Laggan were made very uneasy and many of the disbanded planters joined Coote's army in Derry.[79] Coote marched to Letterkenny and Bishop McMahon decided to give battle on 21 June at the ford of Scarriffhollis on the river Swilly. After an initial hard fight in which the Laggan troops participated, McMahon's estimated force of 3,000 were routed and almost annihilated in a vicious pursuit.[80] It is likely that over 2,500 of the Ulster Irish soldiers were killed in the battle. The native nobility of the province were also almost wiped out with Owen Roe O'Neill's son Henry being among the notable casualties. Many of the Gaelic officers were executed after they surrendered. One of the few Donegal soldiers at the battle Captain Owen O'Doherty, a commander of a troop of horse in Henry O'Neill's regiment, survived the massacre.[81] Mulmurry McSweeney was also fortunate that he had asked Bishop McMahon before the battle for permission to march off with his regiment and attempt to capture Doe castle 'for their future security in that part of the country'.[82]

After the battle of Scarriffhollis, John son of old Hugh Boy O'Donnell is noted amongst the Ulster Gaelic leadership.[83] The last organized units of the Ulster army surrendered to the Cromwellians in April 1653 and it is probably around this time that John left for Spain. According to bardic poetry John O'Donnell died in 1655.[84] By now large areas of Ireland were in the grip of a serious guerrilla war as Gaelic bandits and demobilized Catholic soldiers took to the mountains and began to attack local settlers and small bodies of Cromwellian troops.[85] These guerrilla fighters were called Tories from the Irish word *tóraigh* (to hunt or pursue). Although Co. Donegal was not one of the worst affected areas, the islands off the west coast of the county became the base of a prominent Tory, James Crone O'Donnell. In March 1653, James Crone, who is called in a letter from an English sea captain 'a bloody rebel', seized two English ships as they sheltered off the Rosses. O'Donnell had already captured another ship and kept English captives 'in miserable slavery'. However, Captain Humfelsted of the ship the Marigold fitted out a boat with a cannon and 50 sailors, surprised James Crone's little fleet of captured ships, released the prisoners and broke up the Donegal band of Tories.[86] Local folklore states that James Crone O'Donnell was eventually captured and executed at Lifford.[87] More definite information survives for the nobles Turlough McCaffar O'Donnell and Mulmurry McSweeney, who were deeply implicated in the events of 1641. They were exempted from 'pardon for life and estate' in 1652.[88] Mulmurry McSweeney was put on trial in Dublin for the murder of Robert Atkins in 1641. Nevertheless, he was acquitted and went into exile abroad.[89] Eventually Cromwellian forces pacified the entire county and after the war even installed a garrison in the 'little castle' on remote Tory Island 'commanded by a Governor and a ward of the State soldiers'.[90]

With the running to ground of the Tories in the Rosses and the outlawing of the last leaders of the Gaelic nobility, an uneasy exhausted peace descended on Co. Donegal. The bitterness of over a decade of warfare left an enduring legacy of hatred and resentment in the county. It would be a very long time, well into the 18th century before the settlers of Donegal could forgive and forget the rebellion of the Gaelic Irish in 1641. A large number of people had been killed in the county and the wounds of this war would take a very long time to heal.

3. Confiscation and restoration but a second 'times of trouble'[1]

The area of Co. Donegal most affected by the wars of the 1640s and early 1650s was the barony of Kilmacrennan. Stretching from the river Swilly to the Atlantic coast, this was the only part of Donegal where Gaelic and settler landowners lived side by side. As a result the human and material destruction was extensive. A survey of Co. Donegal dating from the mid-1650s records the 'burnt castle' of Ramelton, the large house at Drum in the parish of Mevagh (belonging to the settler Dutton family) 'burnt in the late war' and the island of Downmcfracky situated near Moyross, 'which in time of war was made use of by the natives for strength, being naturally fortified'.[2] Parts of the barony of Raphoe stretching from upper Glenfinn to the village of Ballindrait had also been extensively plundered during the war with ruined castles and planter houses dotting the countryside.[3] This was also an area of Co. Donegal where settlers and natives lived adjacent to each other. Niall Garbh O'Donnell's family had remained in the valley after the plantation although they no longer owned any land. However, areas adjacent to destroyed parts of the county survived the war virtually intact, for example the small town of Letterkenny and the village of Newtown Cunningham. In the mid-1650s Letterkenny was described as a bustling town with 'a market every Friday, and two fairs in the year, with a large dwelling stone house having a bawn of four flankers, a fair church and a bridge at the end of the said town over the said river of Swilly'. Similarly Newtown Cunningham, although attacked by the garrison of Derry in 1649, had by the mid-1650s recovered and after the war retained its bridge and 'a pretty house and bawn and a little village enjoyed at present by the coheirs of Sir John Cunningham knight'.[4]

The 1641 rebellion and the subsequent years of warfare were a disaster for the Gaelic Irish nobility of Co. Donegal. Every single Catholic in the county who owned land in 1641 had their estates confiscated by the Cromwellians. The forfeitures included the large estate of Turlough O'Boyle, the medium-sized estates of the sons and widow of Donal Gorm McSweeney (Donal Óg, Hugh Boy and Honora McSweeney), and the substantial lands of the family of Walter McSweeney, led by his son Everden McSweeney (the JP), and Walter's widow, Gráinne O'Gallagher.[5] These nobles do not appear to have been involved in the original plotting which led to the outbreak of the rebellion in October 1641, but O'Boyle went on to become a leading

Confederate politician and adherent of General O'Neill. Other nobles such as Mulmurry McSweeney and Turlough McCaffar O'Donnell who held small estates in 1641 were more deeply implicated in the events of 1641 and as has already been stated not only forfeited their land but were also sentenced to death if captured.[6] In all, around 20 Gaelic Catholic nobles forfeited their estates in Co. Donegal to the Cromwellians. However, three McSweeneys in the barony of Kilmacrennan saved their small estates by converting to Protestantism and thus as 'Irish Protestants' were allowed to retain their holdings.[7]

The settlers in Donegal after the war appear to have been naturally very hostile to the remaining Gaelic nobles in the county. Discrimination was rife against the Gaelic Irish (and possibly also against the Ulster Scots), well into the 1670s. For example, in 1677 in the measures 'to be employed towards the relief of the poor inhabitants of Letterkenny', it was stipulated that 'English inhabitants of the town to be preferred'.[8] This and similar incidents obviously stemmed from the bitterness and hatred engendered by the war. As a result, the O'Donnells of Glenfinn were driven out of the county and migrated to find refuge in Co. Mayo. The family of Niall Garbh O'Donnell, now led by his grandson Rory of Lifford, settled at Ballycroy near Blacksod Bay. Rory was followed by a large number of native families from Glenfinn who settled with him in Mayo.[9] The family of Niall Garbh's brother Hugh Boy O'Donnell also migrated to Co. Mayo and settled in the Castlebar region. The head of the family, Hugh Boy's son John died in Spain in 1655 and the family seems to have been led at the time by John's wife, Catherine O'Rourke. It is clear that the family did find a home here as it is later recorded that John and Catherine's son Hugh was 'bred in these parts from his infancy, [and] was perfectly acquainted with the country'.[10] In fact, there appears to have been a mass movement of the O'Donnells of Glenfinn to Co. Mayo after the war as Calvagh Roe O'Donnell, the leader of the family of Niall Garbh's brother Conn Óg (d. 1601) also settled near Castlebar at this time.[11] As a result of the war and this migration the Gaelic natives of Co. Donegal were left leaderless, landless and poverty stricken. Bishop O'Cullinane, probably the last substantial Gaelic noble from the county died in exile in Spanish Flanders in 1661.[12]

After the Restoration of King Charles II in 1660 there appears to have been a brief moment of optimism amongst many of the dispossessed nobility of Co. Donegal. Colonel Mulmurry McSweeney returned from exile to Donegal and as an important local Royalist figure took the lead in representing the Gaelic Irish nobles of the county who felt they had a case for having their small estates returned to them. In December 1660 Mulmurry submitted 'The humble petition of Colonel Mulmurry McSweeney, Major Niall McSweeney and the rest of the officers and soldiers late of their regiment in his Majesty's service in Ireland and the widows and orphans to them belonging whose names are hereunto annexed'.[13] The attached document contained a list of McSweeney's adherents including two of his officers and ten soldiers or their families, one of them being the son of a Captain O'Donnell killed fighting in the Royalist army at the battle of Rathmines (fought outside Dublin in August 1649). Colonel McSweeney also represented a large group of widows and children, mostly from the McSweeney families. Mulmurry's list grouped these Gaelic nobles under headings entitled 'The names of such widows aforesaid, whose husbands deceased before the wars', and 'The names of the orphans that were under age in 1641 and never in arms till the year 1648'. One young noble, Daniel McSweeney was said not to have been 'full five years in 1641', while Eleanor McSweeney's husband was 'deceased long before the wars'. McSweeney's petition further stated that 'All the said persons and parcels lie in the barony of Kilmacrennan and County of Donegal viz Tír Chonaill'.[14]

Colonel McSweeney protested the loyalty and Royalist sympathies of himself and his followers who 'hath cheerfully submitted unto and really prosecuted the peace concluded by his grace the duke of Ormond (then Lord Lieutenant of Ireland), with your Majesty's Catholics of the said kingdom in the year 1648'. McSweeney stressed 'the loss of sundry of their officers and soldiers' who had been killed fighting for the Royalists 'until the said kingdom was overpowered'. Mulmurry also added that all the land he was petitioning for 'their several estates not exceeding yearly £200 or thereabouts none of your said petitioners receiving lands or decrees in Connacht or county of Clare, and which pittances of lands remaining indisposed of to Adventurers or soldiers'. McSweeney and his followers feared underhand dealings in the Court of Claims where some of the court officials were alleged to 'have surreptitiously obtained a grant of the said lands amongst other lands of the county of Donegal most unjustly pretending it forfeit and to be theirs'.[15] Certainly both Bishop Leslie of Raphoe and Oliver Fitzwilliam, who King Charles II created earl of Tyrconnell, both claimed the confiscated lands of the McSweeneys and Turlough O'Boyle after the Restoration.[16]

The petition was examined 'At the Court at Whitehall', on 10 December 1660 by King Charles himself. Although nearly all the Donegal people represented in the petition claimed very small estates, most of only one quarter of land, the king's administration was concerned by the number claiming land as 'the petition concerned many and doth depend upon several particulars'.[17] In the end only Colonel McSweeney, whom the king's officials regarded as 'signally merited of your Majesty's most Royal Father, and your Majesty for his faithfulness and fidelity', may have recovered his mother's small estate due to his services to the Royalists after 1648.[18] The rest of the Donegal cases seem to have been kept for the subsequent Court of Claims.

The Court of Claims eventually sat from February 1663 to August 1663. When he returned to his kingdoms of Britain and Ireland in 1660 Charles II made a declaration that any Catholics who had fought for the Royalists, or who had lost their land merely because of their religion, were to have their estates restored to them. No land was to be returned to Catholic nobles who were in rebellion before 1643, or who had been Confederate Catholics before 1648, or who had been of General O'Neill's party in 1649. This would have included a number of Gaelic Donegal landowners, but not the majority of them.[19] However, no Catholic Gaelic Irish landowner from Co. Donegal apart possibly from Colonel McSweeney regained their lands. There was a clause at the Court of Claims, which stated that no land was to be returned to those who 'enjoyed his estate in the rebels' quarters (being of full age and sound memory)', which would have included nearly all the Gaelic Irish nobles of Donegal no matter what they did during the war. The Gaelic nobles of Donegal mostly had held very small estates and wielded no influence at court. Apart from Mulmurry McSweeney's petition of 1660 little representation seems to have been made on their behalf. Also, the Court of Claims simply ran out of time. Cases were taken in strict order with Ulster being the third province to be heard, and Donegal being the last county of that province. In the end it does not appear that any of the cases of the Gaelic Irish of Donegal were even heard by the Court of Claims. From the start the British Crown authorities in Ireland knew that there was not enough land available to restore all of the innocent landowners. King Charles had also stated that the Cromwellian landowners would be able to keep their lands and the time given to the Court of Claims to hear the cases was deliberately kept short. Many Gaelic nobles from Co. Donegal must have been unjustly deprived of having their lands restored to them. In 1666 two of these nobles, Manus O'Donnell and Daniel McSweeney, signed a Catholic Declaration drafted in March of that year. This declaration put on record for King Charles II, the disgust felt by many of his Irish Catholic subjects at the bribery and other chicanery which had dominated the Court of Claims, where 'the claimant who had the heaviest purse and perhaps a lame cause must be first heard, and the poor let him be never so innocent not permitted to come to a hearing'.[20]

After the Restoration, land ownership in Donegal even amongst the settler population continued to be uncertain for a very long time. A legal dispute over ownership of the largest estate in the west of the county, that of the earl of Annandale in Boylagh and Banagh, broke out in 1659 and was to last into the 1690s. As the estate has been discussed already in this book, the events surrounding it at the time of the Restoration in 1660 are worthy of close examination. James Murray, the second earl of Annandale, died in December 1658 without any heirs. Murray left his very extensive estate in Boylagh and Banagh to a distant relative, Richard Murray of Broughton, who was a minor landlord (laird) in lowland Scotland. However, from 1659, a rival nobleman, Sir Robert Creighton, laid claim to the estate, which created litigation and various attempts to seize ownership over a period of 30 years. Sir Robert claimed the estate in the Irish Court of Chancery by virtue of 'a supposed will of the earl of 8 December 1658, the day of his death'.[21] Creighton's claim was also based upon his assertion that 'James, late earl of Annandale', willed him the estate 'having a particular affection for respondent, his near kinsman, to whom moreover he owed £5,000 by Scotch bonds, besides loans of £2,200 to other persons, for most of which respondent stood bound with him'.[22] Creighton changed his name to Murray and travelled to Co. Donegal in 1659 and seized control of the Annandale estates. When the case came to court in February 1660 though, the jury found in favour of Richard Murray. Murray came to Donegal to live on the estate and resided at Killybegs until 1672, when he and his family returned to Scotland and became absentee landlords.[23]

The uncertainty of ownership of the lands of Boylagh and Banagh continued. In 1667 Sir Albert Cunningham of Mount Charles, a relation of the Murrays of Broughton and a prominent Donegal landowner in his own right, bought a large portion of the estate in Boylagh from Richard Murray for £4,500. In the ensuing years Cunningham began to improve the lands 'and laid out to the value of the estate in improvements'.[24] However, in 1678 Creighton again challenged ownership and had some success in the Scottish courts leading to the Irish Court of Chancery admitting 'the Scotch decree as evidence of forgery and decreed accordingly, without examining any new witnesses and left the validity of the will to be tried on an action to recover possession'.[25] In 1687 Creighton sought possession of the estate and in December of that year the high sheriff of Donegal and his under sheriffs gave possession 'of every house and cottage, small and great' in Boylagh and Banagh to Creighton, which the local population accepted 'for fear'.[26] The dispute ended up in the English house of lords in 1691–2 when Sir Albert Cunningham's son Henry took a 'petition and appeal' against Sir Robert Creighton. Although the dispute ran from the late 1650s to the early 1690s Creighton's case was based upon very flimsy grounds. It was alleged that the will he obtained from the earl on the day of his death 'was made by a little scrivener in Westminster; two apothecary's boys were witnesses',[27] which suggests that Creighton took advantage of the dying earl. In the end, the Broughton Murrays and Henry Cunningham won the case upon the payment of a composition and the entire estate was eventually rented by Henry from the Murrays.[28] The winning of the dispute was very expensive, and cost Cunningham '1,200 guineas' (a guinea was worth 21 shillings), which left him in debt and 'very scarce of money'. The legal uncertainty over these years on the Murray estates also unsettled the Protestant freeholders who began to claim that Henry Cunningham had 'no possession'. This led Henry to write to Lady Broughton in 1694 of the 'many other difficulties I meet with from some of your tenants and my near relatives who are so perverse in everything that relates to either your interest or mine that I have found as much difficulty in managing them as I did in carrying our cases, for they are so far from paying what was proposed to them on account of the suit that they neither give thanks to me that saved them from ruin nor will pay a farthing rent but what is extorted from them by the collector of the crown rent'.[29]

Even though the Gaelic population of Donegal had been reduced to a very poor condition, by the 1670s it was recovering. After the death of Eoin O'Cullinane, the bishop of Raphoe in 1661, no one replaced him. There were vicars general of the diocese; Hugh O'Gallagher was appointed vicar general in 1657 and Luke Plunkett (most likely not a native of the diocese) was vicar general in 1671.[30] There were also prominent local people descended from dispossessed nobles who continued to live in the county although they now had little power or wealth. They were still accorded traditional respect. Small sets of Irish annals continued to be kept in Donegal at this time and an entry in one of them records how the descendant of one important Donegal noble family, although now living in Co. Mayo, left for Spain with letters of recommendation from some of the most important Gaelic nobles and Catholic churchmen of the county. The annals state:

> Hugh O'Donnell son of John son of Hugh Boy son of Conn son of the Calvagh went to Spain in this year and fulsome devoted letters with him from the nobles and high gentlemen of Tír Chonaill and most of the province of Ulster both church and country to the king of Spain declaring for him, and his paternity, and received as a result of this installation as earl of Tír Chonaill as his ancestors received before together with a great pension and respect from the king of Spain.[31]

Hugh O'Donnell states that he was 'born in Donegal in Ireland', but had been living near Castlebar with his mother Catherine O'Rourke and his brother Conal since the end of the war in 1653.[32] Hugh's grandfather Hugh Boy O'Donnell, a brother of Niall Garbh, had been a prominent figure and the family may have thought it prudent to leave Donegal after the war. This branch of the O'Donnells obviously had sufficient prestige to continue to be held in high regard by the Gaelic inhabitants of their original county. When he arrived in Spain the Spanish began to call Hugh O'Donnell, the earl of Tir Chonaill. This was largely an honorary title as Hugh had no claim to the title by descent and even had O'Donnell relatives in Co. Mayo, Niall Garbh's family, who were senior to him. By 1674 O'Donnell was a captain in the Spanish cavalry and he soon became a respected Spanish officer. By 1684 Hugh had been promoted to colonel and commanded his own regiment or tercio of Irish infantry. In June 1684 the Spanish ambassador in London, on behalf of the Spanish King, requested permission from King Charles II for O'Donnell to recruit for his regiment in Ireland. Charles issued an order 'permitting and authorizing the said Don Hugo O'Donnell, or such officers as he shall appoint to levy recruits in that Our kingdom for the said regiment, and to transport them into Spain'.[33]

In February 1685 Charles II, king of Britain and Ireland, died and his Catholic brother succeeded him as James II. The accession of King James II to the British throne threw his Irish kingdom into turmoil. James, being a Catholic monarch, threatened to overturn the settler interest on the island as the king's Catholic subjects sought positions of power and influence in the new administration. In Co. Donegal one of the first powerful settlers to suffer at the hands of the new regime was Sir Albert Cunningham of Mount Charles. In December 1660 Cunningham had been appointed lieutenant general of the ordinance in Ireland by Charles II for service to the Royalist cause during the civil wars which had cost Sir Albert 'the loss of his blood and the impairing of his fortune by frequent imprisonments'. Soon after James became king 'some person lately by misinformation' secured Cunningham's replacement by a Captain John Giles by telling the new king that Sir Albert was 'very old and infirm' and needed to be retired. Sir Albert petitioned King James writing to the king: 'That your petitioner is most confident and fully assured that it is not your gracious majesty's inclination nor intention to hurt any person who has served the Crown loyally and constantly, to gratify any person who has not done so'.[34] When the king ignored Cunningham's petition he alienated one of the most prominent Royalist settlers in Co. Donegal.

Almost immediately James II's succession led to great uncertainty in Ireland over land ownership as the dispossessed Gaelic Irish and Old English sought the return of their lands lost in the 1650s. King James appointed a number of Gaelic nobles to positions of power in Donegal. Conal O'Donnell, a grandson of old Hugh Boy O'Donnell and a brother of Colonel Hugh O'Donnell in the Spanish army was made lord lieutenant of Co. Donegal.[35] Conal had been living in Co. Mayo but returned to his native county. James also appointed Manus O'Donnell, Turlough Óg O'Boyle and Daniel O'Donnell as deputy lieutenants of the county. Manus O'Donnell was from Boylagh and received a commission in the Jacobite army.[36] Daniel O'Donnell also received an army commission.[37] Daniel, who was born in 1665, was a son of Turlough McCaffar O'Donnell and a distant kinswoman, Joanne O'Donnell, whom Turlough married late in life.[38] Daniel later stated that his father and his elder half-brother (Hugh Boy) had commanded the Tír Chonaill regiment during the wars of the 1640s.[39] Manus and Daniel O'Donnell were also appointed aldermen of the city of Derry.[40] The rising expectations of the Gaelic Irish in Donegal naturally led to fear and unease amongst the settler landowners and wider settler population. As one contemporary settler author, the clergyman John MacKenzie, put it:[41] 'There were but too strong grounds to suspect a general design of the Irish papists against the British Protestants, and particularly of the Ultoghs who had given the earliest demonstration of their cruel disposition in the rebellion of 1641'. The wealthy began to send their families to the safety of England or Scotland, and those that remained behind began to arm themselves and organize militarily for defence. William Stewart, the baron of Ramelton (and also Viscount Mountjoy), raised a regiment of infantry amongst the settlers of north Donegal and Sir Albert Cunningham raised a regiment of dragoons in the south of the county.[42] When a section of Stewart's force was sent to reinforce the city of Derry and he himself sent on a diplomatic mission to France, where he was imprisoned in the Bastille, it left the settlers in the north of the county isolated.[43] However, towns such as Rathmullan continued to be garrisoned.

When King James was deposed by William of Orange in November 1688 the settler towns of Derry and Enniskillen in west Ulster became centres of support for the new King. The two towns refused to recognize James' administration and as in 1641 began to organize militarily as the rift between the Catholic king and his Protestant subjects widened. Thousands of settlers and their families took refuge in Derry fearing Jacobite reprisals, many of these being from the Laggan and further afield in Donegal. Albert Cunningham and his regiment cooperated with the rebel forces in Enniskillen led by Gustavus Hamilton. Sir Albert based himself where he could support the towns of Donegal, Ballyshannon and Killybegs. In early 1689 Hamilton put a garrison into Doe castle. The castle was soon captured by one of the McSweeneys, who was referred to at the time as 'a Tory', a sure indication that disorder was spreading in Co. Donegal.[44]

King James landed in Ireland in March 1689 and dispatched an army north to capture Derry and bring the rebels of the north-west to heel. The settlers attempted to create a large force of all their able-bodied men and hold the line of the river Finn against the Jacobite army. The plan collapsed in disorder and the planters fled in the face of the Jacobite troops and sought refuge in Derry. The Jacobite army besieging Derry set up its headquarters in St Johnston in the Laggan. A Jacobite camp was also located in Glenfinn to keep off any raiders from Enniskillen and south Donegal and a large force was sent through the pass of Bearnas Mór to attack Sir Albert Cunningham. Donegal town was burnt, although the castle held out and 1,500 cattle and sheep were taken.[45] On 30 June 1689, Marshal Von Rosen, a senior French advisor at Derry ordered that thousands of the local settlers and their families, many of whom were from the Laggan, be driven in front of the city walls in order to intimidate the garrison into surrender. The troops in Derry threatened to execute their Jacobite prisoners in reprisal and the hostages were let go.[46] Panic spread in the Laggan as a result of this action and many thousands of settlers took refuge on Inch Island in Lough Swilly. The island was soon defended by the sailors of a Williamite fleet, which was attempting to sail up the river Foyle to the relief of Derry.[47] The Williamites planted 16 cannon on Inch and also placed two gun-ships between the island and the Inishowen shore.

At the same time as the siege of Derry was being conducted, King James' parliament met at Dublin. There were no MPs from Co. Donegal, due to the fact that the county was either in the hands of the settlers or the scene of actual warfare. James' parliament passed an Act of Attainder outlawing as traitors and confiscating the estates of over 2,000 rebel landowners who had refused to recognize James' government. Heading the list of attainted rebels for Co. Donegal were Henry Cunningham of Mount Charles (probably an error for his father Sir Albert), and Gustavus Hamilton of Rosguill, in addition to many others, 'all late of the County of Donegal'.[48] When the siege of Derry failed at the end of July 1689 and the Jacobite army retreated, the plantation towns of the Laggan were set on fire and destroyed. It was at this time that the bishop's palace at Raphoe was burnt down.[49] However, not many settlers had been killed in this the greatest threat ever experienced by the plantation community in Co. Donegal. In 1689 the loss to the settlers of Co. Donegal was more material, with the destruction of their homes and villages and the carrying off of their livestock. With the retreat of the Jacobite army from Co. Donegal the Jacobite administration also fled as Conal O'Donnell, the lord lieutenant of the county, left for Co. Mayo.

Conal's brother, Colonel Hugh O'Donnell returned to Ireland from Spain in order to join the Jacobites in July 1690. Arriving just after the Jacobite defeat at the Boyne, O'Donnell's landing created something of a sensation as messianic prophesies began to be associated with him as it was believed that he would win a great victory over the English at Singland Hill near Limerick.[50] It is not clear if Colonel O'Donnell instigated the prophecies in relation to himself but he soon began to call himself Balldearg (red spotted), from a prophesied birthmark.[51] As O'Donnell 'went away privately out of Spain into Portugal', and sailed for Ireland without official permission, he published a manifesto in Portugal to justify his actions.[52] O'Donnell stated that 'It is almost a century since the ruin of my house began', but that now 'the present constitution of the British kingdom offers almost certain hopes for restoring myself (if not completely) in some respectable part of my estates'. O'Donnell believed that as the settlers of Co. Donegal 'being possessed at present of the estates of my House', were 'those who with most obstinacy have revealed themselves to be against his Majesty in Ireland', their lands 'have to come into the king's hands', and that as a result 'it is not doubtful that he will restore some part to the legitimate heirs, who should be found at present in his service'.[53] Although O'Donnell quickly met King James and his lord lieutenant in Ireland, Richard Talbot, the duke of Tyrconnell, and was promoted to brigadier and authorized to raise a small force to guard the upper Shannon, he was always regarded with suspicion by the Jacobite authorities. This eventually led O'Donnell to open negotiations with the Williamites after the Jacobite administration began to blame Hugh for the loss of Galway city. Galway fell to the Williamites after the battle of Aughrim fought in July 1691, when an attempt by O'Donnell to reinforce the city failed. During his time in north Connacht, many Gaelic refugees from Ulster along with their creaghts attached themselves to O'Donnell's army, just as the population of the province had followed General O'Neill's army in the 1640s. The Dutch General Godard

Ginkel gave O'Donnell terms that his followers could have a pardon and general amnesty, and 'free leave to go to those parts of the kingdom where they dwelt before the war', and that Hugh himself could retain a brigade of 3,000 to be transported to serve in the Spanish army in Flanders.[54] General Ginkel, had a high opinion of O'Donnell and hoping to end the war quickly he sent a letter to O'Donnell stating that 'it was against his inclination to force a man of honour to turn bandit on the mountains, where he must at last infallibly perish'.[55] Ginkel also wrote to King William that: 'The Brigadier Balldearg O'Donnell, having with him 3,000 Ulstermans, has made proposals to me for submitting; ... I beg you to consider that the submission of this man would add much to the peace of the country, and that the people of Ulster, have great confidence in him'.[56]

O'Donnell later joined Sir Albert Cunningham and 150 of his dragoons at Castlebar in late August 1691. Cunningham too formed a high opinion of O'Donnell and regarded Hugh as 'a man of reason'.[57] In early September O'Donnell's men began to assist Cunningham's regiment against the Jacobite garrison in Sligo by stopping supplies being taken into the town from the surrounding countryside.[58] However, on the morning of 5 September, O'Donnell's and Cunningham's camp at Collooney was attacked by the Jacobites from Sligo. Utilizing a 'great fog' the Jacobites 'were amongst our tents before we were any way prepared'. Twenty of Cunningham's dragoons were killed and all their equipment seized. When Sir Albert attempted to mount his horse, it was 'unruly and broke away and in spite of what we could do, was made prisoner and carried off'.[59] Sir Albert was later killed by the Jacobites. As 'most of O'Donnell's regiment [was] sent into the country for provisions', Balldearg was almost captured himself and it was stated that he 'escaped the nearest that ever man did from being taken and if they had got him he had been presently hanged'.[60]

The Williamite War ended in Co. Donegal with the main settler area of the Laggan plundered and burnt by the Jacobite army in 1689. The planter towns of Donegal and Rathmullan had also been burnt down by this army in 1689. The vast majority of the settler population had survived although some important leaders such as Sir Albert Cunningham were killed during the war. Co. Donegal was in a disturbed state for many years after the war particularly its western parts. In December 1694 three Tories, Murrough McSweeney, Turlough Mc Fadden and Patrick McColin were still 'on their keeping' and a reward of £10 was offered for their heads.[61] Undoubtedly there was natural anger amongst the settler community directed at the Gaelic Irish population of the west of the county as a result of the incursion of the Jacobite army into the Laggan in 1689. The leaders of this army were King James himself, major French officers and Jacobite leaders from outside the county. The O'Donnell nobles who rose to prominence in the county administration under the Jacobites such as Conal, Daniel and Manus O'Donnell were not major figures.

Manus was killed at the Battle of Aughrim. Daniel O'Donnell left for France after the Jacobite surrender at Limerick, bringing with him the medieval relic associated with the armies of the lordship of Tír Chonaill, the Cathach.[62] Brigadier Hugh Balldearg O'Donnell probably never saw himself seriously taking over the old O'Donnell lordship of Tír Chonaill, even though he was occasionally called the earl of Tír Chonaill in Spain. Brigadier O'Donnell most likely returned to Ireland to recruit troops for Spanish service and perhaps make a name for himself in the war. He acquitted himself well during his campaign in Connacht and the Gaelic people of Ireland seem to have forgiven him for joining the Williamites. He returned to Spain in 1695 to continue his successful career in the Spanish army. There was little or no Catholic land in Co. Donegal even before the war left to confiscate, but there are hints that the settlers again turned on any Gaelic nobles left in Co. Donegal after 1692 and eventually drove most of them out of the county.[63]

Conclusion

Co. Donegal in 1610 was an overwhelmingly Gaelic territory with a very small number of English and Scottish soldiers and ecclesiastics present within the county. The county presented a ruined appearance following the end of the Nine Years War in 1603 and the O'Doherty revolt in 1608. The population was also largely leaderless due to the flight of the earls in 1607 and the events of 1608. By 1710 the appearance of the entire county had been transformed. The eastern part of Donegal, the Laggan territory and southern Inishowen resembled a piece of lowland Scotland transferred into Ireland. There were thousands of settler families now inhabiting this area and a well developed network of little plantation towns and villages stretching from Newtown Cunningham, St Johnston and Lifford west to Letterkenny, Ramelton and Rathmullan.[1] The south of the county also had a substantial settler population in the towns of Ballyshannon and Donegal. There had been a total transformation in landownership from 1610 to 1710. In 1610, most land in Co. Donegal was held by Gaelic Irish nobles, even if title to these lands was somewhat unsettled due to the earl of Tír Chonaill's attempted land reforms and his flight to the continent. The only British outsiders holding land were the Protestant bishop of Raphoe, George Montgomery, and a small number of soldiers. By 1710 almost 100 per cent of the land of Co. Donegal was in settler hands – that of the established church, Trinity College Dublin and the descendants of the original undertakers and servitors and other British noblemen who had bought into Co. Donegal or been granted land by Charles II. The only land left to the Gaelic nobility was that of the descendants of three of the McSweeneys who had converted to Protestantism to save their estates. By the beginning of the 18th century there was not one Catholic Gaelic landowner in Co. Donegal. This was quite unusual even for the Ireland of the time, but was a situation similar to that in many of Donegal's neighbouring counties in Ulster.

The population of Co. Donegal in 1710 was also substantially larger than it had been in 1610. The settlers in east Donegal especially had transformed much of the landscape, draining large bogs, felling woodland and building new roads, bridges and causeways where none existed before.[2] The plantation settlement in east Donegal was the most successfully settled area within the entire six official counties of the Ulster plantation. By 1710 it contained the densest area of Protestant settlement in Ulster outside Down and Antrim. The firm roots of this success were laid by the conscientious undertakers of the

1610s and 1620s such as Ludovic Stuart, the duke of Lennox, Bishop Andrew Knox and the Cunninghams of Ayrshire. The early consolidation of the plantation in Co. Donegal was greatly helped by the fact that many of the undertakers were from the same parts of lowland Scotland, particularly the Ayrshire region. Hundreds of families were settled in Co. Donegal, and they transformed the Laggan area especially into a prosperous and well governed territory. There was land hunger in lowland Scotland during this period and this led many settlers to plant in east Donegal. The building of the fortified city at Derry also greatly assisted in the building of the Laggan plantation, as east Donegal became the natural hinterland for the town. The plantation was less successful in other parts of the county. There was substantial settlement in parts of Tirhugh around the towns of Ballyshannon and Donegal and along the western shore of Lough Swilly. The mountainous interior and Gaelic west of the county was very lightly settled indeed. Here major landowners such as John Murray the earl of Annandale, who was the largest landholder in Co. Donegal outside of Inishowen during the 1620s and 30s, was more interested in harnessing the revenues from the lucrative fisheries on the rivers which flowed through his land or that existed offshore. Murray brought in very few Scottish or English settlers.

The settlers of east and south Donegal were very fortunate in October 1641 that their Gaelic Irish neighbours hesitated for a number of weeks before joining the revolt of the rest of the Ulster Irish. This allowed the settlers to join with those planters of west Tyrone who had also survived the first rebel onslaught. The Laggan army formed from the man folk of these settlers played a prominent role in the subsequent warfare of the 1640s. There appears to have been a massacre of a small number of settlers near Doe castle in west Donegal, followed by the destruction of plantation houses in this area, attacks which continued into December 1641. However, many of the settler areas of Co. Donegal survived virtually unscathed. Again the decision of the Cromwellians to leave the Donegal settler landowners in situ was also very fortunate as this act served to consolidate the Donegal plantation rather than fracture it by dispersal of these men throughout Ireland. This occurred even though most of the Scottish settlers in Co. Donegal had supported the covenanters in Scotland and then Charles II. In 1688 many of the Donegal settlers rebelled against King James II and assisted in the defence of Derry city in 1689 against James' Jacobite army. Although the Laggan area and a number of settler towns were burnt and plundered by the Jacobite army that besieged the city of Derry, the majority of settlers survived either within the walls of Derry or on Inch Island, which was well fortified by a Williamite fleet. There were no massacres of settlers in Donegal during this conflict and much of the south of the county remained in settler hands throughout the war.

The planted areas of Co. Donegal saw extensive development and land improvement and should be considered quite prosperous by 1710. Evidence survives though to suggest that the settlers of Donegal had some major problems by the beginning of the 18th century. Although from a lightly planted area, the correspondence of Henry Cunningham in the 1690s and early 1700s records evidence of a shortage of money and non-payment of rent in the west of the county. In 1701, Cunningham recorded 'the poverty of this unhappy kingdom', there being 'a £1,000 rent now owing me and some of it for two years'.[3] Henry began to accept payments of cattle and butter in lieu of money rents.[4] The information recorded by Henry Cunningham points to a depressed market in early 18th-century Ireland which may owe much to the aftermath of the Williamite War. The completion of the planting of all the available good land in Donegal may also have been accomplished by 1710. This, coupled with the depressed economic situation, led to the beginning of the emigration of many settler families to the American colonies. In 1729 a ship docked at Killybegs 'belonging to New England' which took away 'as many passengers as she can carry'.[5] Later in July 1729 two more ships called into Killybegs and sailed away with 'some 300 tenants and several other gentlemen tenants'.[6] Nevertheless, despite these problems the plantation in Co. Donegal by 1710 was a major success and achievement when compared to the situation in the county after the end of the Nine Years War.

The inauguration stone of the O'Donnell chieftains survived in the ruins of the Franciscan abbey in Kilmacrennan for a long period, as a relic of the vanished power of the lords of Tír Chonaill. It was eventually 'destroyed by a Mr McSweeney, who having changed his religion, became a violent hater of everything Irish'.[7] The wealth and status of the Gaelic Irish population of Co. Donegal steadily declined throughout the 17th century. The initial plantation in 1610 came as a rude shock to many of the Gaelic nobles of the O'Donnell lordship, quite a number of whom received no estates. In the 1650s the descendants of those who had received land in the plantation also lost their lands due to the outbreak of the rebellion in 1641. By 1660 there was possibly only one Gaelic Catholic landowner in the county and the status of the Gaelic population had been further reduced to a very low level. Although in the 1700s there were still noble Gaelic families in Donegal such as that of James O'Friel, who was influential enough to have his genealogy recorded in 1744,[8] other noble families such as the McSweeneys of Doe became travelling tinkers, remaining present in Co. Donegal although they no longer retained any land.[9] Gaelic culture survived in west Donegal, in the Rosses and on the offshore islands. In the almost total absence of any settlers in this region the population remained Catholic and Irish speaking. Even the population in the Gaelic west was reduced to a low level of status by 1710. In 1704 Henry Cunningham commented on the poverty of the Gaelic Irish population on his lands stating that 'the misery they are in demands pity more than severity'. In response to the indifferent attitude of his overall absentee landlord, Alexander Murray of Broughton, Cunningham added: 'for my part I can have no hand in sending hundreds of families a begging'.[10] The situation of the Gaelic Irish of Boylagh and Banagh continued to deteriorate, until in 1729 a famine threatened to break out. In that year Murray of Broughton's agent, James Hamilton, recorded that: 'bread is so exceeding dear that famine is feared among the poorer sort'. Hamilton also commented on the harsh uncaring attitude of Alexander Murray, stating 'for you give no ear to it, nor ever takes the least notice of it'.[11]

There was little organized resistance to the Ulster plantation in Co. Donegal. In the early years of the plantation from 1610 to the 1630s the Gaelic Irish population of the county was exhausted and war weary after the end of the Nine Years War in 1603 and the revolt of Sir Cahir O'Doherty in 1608. Disorganized banditry occasionally broke out in the mountainous areas, with companies of woodkerne at large in the 1620s. The fact that the Gaelic Irish of Donegal were bitterly divided amongst themselves after the end of the war must have contributed to the lack of any organized early resistance to the planters. The followers of the earl had remained loyal to the Gaelic confederacy which had fought the Nine Years War, while the adherents of Niall Garbh O'Donnell and Cahir O'Doherty, had fought for the English during the war's final three years. To overthrow the plantation in Co. Donegal after the 1620s once it had established firm roots was going to involve massive loss of life and destruction of property, as was to happen in 1641. Indeed by the 1640s the ability to do this was beyond the Gaelic inhabitants of Donegal.

The émigré community in the Spanish Netherlands surrounding the exiled second earl of Tír Chonaill also desired the overthrow of the plantation in Co. Donegal, although there is little evidence that they actively plotted to destroy it. Hugh Albert O'Donnell was named as one of the proposed leaders of the Irish Republic to be set up once the settlers were defeated in the 1620s plotting of Florence Conry. O'Donnell was not prominent in the planning of this project. The O'Cullinane family was linked to the proposed scheme, but the accusations are most likely false. Hugh Albert O'Donnell does not appear to have had prior knowledge of the outbreak of the 1641 rebellion in Ulster although he did ask the king of Spain for permission to return to Ireland which was refused. When the earl was killed in 1642, the group surrounding him gradually died out.

The Gaelic Irish in Co. Donegal do not appear to have been closely involved in the plotting which preceded the outbreak of the 1641 rebellion either. The Gaelic Irish landowners in the barony of Kilmacrennan were quite isolated from the Irish in the rest of the province, although in the end they were not able to remain aloof from the rebellion as the Irish in Inishowen were able to do. The late involvement of the Donegal Gaelic Irish in the 1641 revolt was a disaster. It allowed the settlers in the county to organize the Laggan army and defeat them in 1642, and subsequently led to the almost complete destruction of the remaining Gaelic landowning community after the Cromwellian conquest in 1653. After the end of the conquest the general Gaelic population was again exhausted by over a decade of bitter warfare. There was a band of Tories at large in west Donegal in the 1650s, but they were ruthlessly suppressed. A few Gaelic nobles survived in Co. Donegal in a reduced condition as tenants. A small number joined the Jacobite cause in the 1680s, again possibly in the hope of improving their fortunes in the county and reversing some of the aspects of the plantation. However, with the exception of Hugh Balldearg O'Donnell, these men were not prominent figures. After the end of the Williamite War in the 1690s there were again a small number of Tories in west Donegal. While the presence of Gaelic bandits in the mountains made travel in some areas dangerous at times, they did not present a major threat to the settlers.

After the end of the Williamite War, memories of the O'Donnell chieftains and the exploits of Balldearg O'Donnell survived in the folklore of the Gaelic Irish population, but there were no longer any substantial leaders from the Gaelic nobility surviving in the county to provide a focus for discontent. The most influential surviving Gaelic nobles from Donegal, the families of Niall Garbh and Hugh Boy O'Donnell, left the county for the province of Connacht in the 1650s. The settler authorities continued to keep a close eye on the Gaelic Irish population of Co. Donegal well into the 1700s. In 1715 a band of seven Torys fled from Co. Fermanagh into the barony of Kilmacrennan. Frederick Hamilton at Lifford was immediately authorized to search for them and raised a posse of around 30 'tolerably armed' settlers.[12] The settlers also kept watch on the few Catholic clergy living amongst the Gaelic population. By the early 1700s there were just over 20 Catholic priests in the entire diocese of Raphoe and a few travelling Franciscan friars.[13] Mass was said in cabins and 'sometimes in the fields' although there were a few mass houses in the very west of the county. There was also a Catholic hedge school hidden in the mountains near Kilmacrennan. No Catholic bishop of Raphoe was appointed from the time of the death of Bishop O'Cullinane in 1661 until James Gallagher was appointed in 1725. In 1731 the British authorities in the county became very anxious to arrest Bishop Gallagher who was a capable, French-educated cleric. In that year they 'applied to the magistrates to have him taken'.[14] A botched attempt to capture the bishop led to the death of a local priest and Gallagher had to go into hiding. This was when he drew up his influential series of sermons which were published in Irish in 1736.[15] Such was the hostility of the settler authorities towards Bishop Gallagher in Co. Donegal that he had to be transferred to the diocese of Kildare in 1737 for his own safety.

By 1710 Co. Donegal had been firmly subdued by the British government and their settlers. The county had been transformed within a century from a warlike, autonomous Gaelic lordship into a well-settled and quite prosperous territory albeit with a largely unplanted west. However, even here the Gaelic population was cowed and leaderless. The settler interest in Co. Donegal had surmounted the difficulties of initial geographic isolation and a hostile, if passive, native population, to put down firm roots quite quickly. The plantation was most successful in the east of the county. It was this firm base which enabled the Donegal plantation to survive the rebellion of the Gaelic Irish of Ulster in 1641 and the campaign of a major Jacobite army in 1689. Although there were divisions amongst the settler population, such as those between some of the Scots of Presbyterian descent and the English of the established church (an early 18th-century Donegal Scots poet from the Laggan spoke of 'Frae the grim craving clergy; How deeply did they charge ye, Wi' fair oppressive tythe?'),[16] by 1710 the settlers in Co. Donegal were so well-entrenched and established that their settlements were now a permanent feature on the Donegal landscape. By the beginning of the 18th century the descendants of the Gaelic nobles who had once ruled the county could only survive outside its borders. A large Gaelic Irish population, the descendants of the original inhabitants of the lordship of Tír Chonaill, continued to live in Co. Donegal in the isolated west.

Notes

ABBREVIATIONS

AFM	*Annals of the Four Masters*, ed. J. O'Donovan (Dublin, 1856).
BAR	*Beatha Aodha Ruaidh Uí Dhomhnaill*, ed. P. Walsh, Part I (London, 1948); Part II (Dublin, 1957).
CSPI	*Calendar of State Papers Ireland.*
DIB	*Dictionary of Irish biography*, ed. J. McGuire and J. Quinn (RIA, 2009).
Hastings MSS	*Report on the manuscripts of the late Reginald Rawdon Hastings* (London, 1947).
HMC	Historical Manuscripts Commission.
IHS	*Irish Historical Studies.*
IMC	Irish Manuscripts Commission.
Inquis. Rot.	*Inquisitionum in Officio Rotulorum Cancellariae Hiberniae Asservatarum.*
Laing MS	*Report on the Laing manuscripts* (London, 1914).
LCS	*Leabhar Chlainne Suibhne*, ed. P. Walsh (Dublin, 1920).
NAI	National Archives of Ireland.
NHI	*New history of Ireland*, ed. T. Moody, F.X. Martin and F.J. Byrne (Oxford, 1976).
NLI	National Library of Ireland.
ODNB	*Oxford dictionary of national biography*, ed. H. Matthew and B. Harrison (Oxford, 2004).
Philad. Papers	*Philadelphia Papers* (*CSPI, 1611–14*).
PRONI	Public Record Office of Northern Ireland.
Salisbury MSS	*Calendar of manuscripts of the most hon. the marquis of Salisbury* (London, 1883–1973).
TNA, SP	Public Record Office State Papers [National Archives, Kew, London].
TNA, SP Dom	Public Record State Papers Domestic [National Archives, Kew, London].
TCD	Trinity College Dublin.
UCD	University College Dublin.
VL	Vatican Library.

INTRODUCTION

1 M. Herity (ed.), *Ordnance Survey letters Donegal* (Dublin, 2000), pp 46–7.

2 Sir Arthur Chichester to the privy council, 12 Sept. 1608, TNA, SP 63/225/184.

3 Sir Thomas Ridgeway, Treasurer of Ireland, to Salisbury, 3 July 1608, TNA, SP 63/224/184.

4 P. Fox to Walsingham, 12 Feb. 1589, TNA, SP 63/141/64; 10 Feb. 1593, TNA, SP 63/173/128; George Bingham, 16 Feb. 1593, TNA, SP 63/173/129.

5 A description of Lough Foyle and the country adjoining endorsed by Sir Henry Docwra, 19 Dec. 1600 TNA, SP 63/207Pt6/221.

6 J. O'Donovan (ed.), 'A narration of the services done ... under me Sir Henry Dowcra' in *Miscellany of the Celtic Society* (Dublin, 1849), p. 258; M. Byrne (ed.), *A history of Ireland in the reign of Elizabeth* (Dublin, 1903), pp 148–9; *AFM*, 1602.

7 Sir Arthur Chichester to the privy council, 12 Sept. 1608, TNA, SP 63/225/184; Sir Henry Folliott to the Lord Deputy, 8 Sept. 1608, TNA, SP 63/225/42.

8 Examination of John Lynshull, Sir Niall O'Donnell's secretary, 15 June 1608, Bodleian Library, Oxford, Carte Papers 61/282; Sir Henry Folliott to the Lord Deputy, 8 Sept. 1608, TNA, SP 63/225/42; The examination of Patrick Óg O'Corcoran, 12 July 1608, *Hastings MSS* IV, pp 157–9.

9 The earl of Tír Chonaill to the Council, 1605, *Salisbury MS* XVII, p. 645.

10 The earl of Tír Chonaill to the earl of Salisbury, 21 May 1606, *Salisbury MS,* XVIII, p. 141.

11 *Inquis. Rot.*, ii 1625–6, Lifford 21 Mar.

12 Bishop Andrew Knox to the lords justices of Ireland, 26 Apr. 1632, TNA, SP 63/253/143.

13 Grant from the king to Rory O'Donnell, 10 Feb. 1603, *Irish Patent Rolls of James I* (Dublin, 1966), p. 13.

14 A note of the grievances of the earl of Tír Chonaill, TNA, SP 63/222/308.

15 The earl of Tír Chonaill to the king, 20 Dec. 1606, *Salisbury MS* XVIII, p. 362.

16 The earl of Tír Chonaill to the earl of Salisbury, After Sept. 1605, *Salisbury MS* XVII, p. 444.

17 *AFM*, 1603.

18 Sir John Davies to Sir Robert Cecil, 19 Apr. 1604, TNA, SP 63/216/15.

19 A note of the grievances of the earl of Tír Chonaill, TNA, SP 63/222/308.

20 Sir Arthur Chichester's instruction to Sir James Ley and Sir John Davies, 14 Oct. 1608, TNA, SP 63/225/225; *Inquis. Rot.*, Appendix V, p. 7.

21 A note of the grievances of the earl of Tír Chonaill, TNA, SP 63/222/308.

22 *Inquis. Rot.*, Appendix V, p. 7.

23 The lord deputy and council to the privy council, 2 Mar. 1607, TNA, SP 63/221/29.

24 Lord Deputy and council to the lords of the council, 21 Jan. 1607, TNA, SP 63/221/7; Sir Arthur Chichester to the earl of Salisbury, 20 Feb. 1607, TNA, SP 63/221/21.

25 Sir Arthur Chichester to Salisbury, 28 Mar. 1607, TNA, SP 63/221/34.

26 Lord Deputy Chichester to the privy council, 16 July 1607, TNA, SP 63/222/101.·

27 Sir Arthur Chichester's instructions to Sir James Ley and Sir John Davies, 14 Oct. 1608, TNA, SP 63/225/225.

28 *Inquis. Rot.*, Appendix V, pp 4–5.

29 The humble petition of Patrick Conley, 1610, TNA, SP 63/232/46.

30 N. Canny, 'The flight of the earls', *IHS* 17 (1970–1), 382.

31 P. Walsh (ed.), *The flight of the earls by Tadhg Ó Cianáin* (Dublin, 1916), pp 8–9.

32 The humble petition of Sir Niall O'Donnell, TNA, SP 63/228/167.

33 Proclamation by the lord deputy and council, 7 Sept. 1607, No. 189, R.R. Steele, *A bibliography of Royal Proclamations of the Tudor and Stuart Sovereigns 1485–1714*, (2 vols, Oxford, 1910), ii p. 18.

34 Sir Arthur Chichester's instructions to Sir James Ley and Sir John Davies, 14 Oct. 1608, TNA, SP 63/225/225.

35 The voluntary confession of Dualtagh McGilduff taken the 8 Mar. 1608, Bodleian Library, Oxford, Carte Papers 61/272.

36 Sir Arthur Chichester's instructions to Sir James Ley and Sir John Davies, 14 Oct. 1608, TNA, SP 63/225/225; Sir Arthur Chichester to Salisbury, 18 Oct. 1608, TNA, SP 63/246/124.

37 *ODNB* 38 (Oxford, 2004), p. 841.

38 *Inquis. Rot.,* ii, Appendix V, pp 1–8.

39 Ibid., pp 4–5.

40 Cambridge UL Add. MS 2766(20)(7), in D. McGettigan, *Red Hugh O'Donnell and the Nine Years War* (Dublin, 2005), pp 132–3.

41 *Inquis. Rot.*, ii, Appendix V, p. 5.

42 Ibid., p. 2

43 *Patent Rolls of James I*, p. 15.

44 Ibid., p. 14.

45 The conveyances made by the earl, Bodleian Library, Oxford, Carte Papers 61/128.

1. THE PLANTATION

1 An abstract of his Majesty's title to the lands in the county of Donegal, Bodleian Library, Oxford, Carte Papers, 61/126.

2 The indictment of Hugh O'Neill, earl of Tyrone, and Rory O'Donnell, earl of Tír Chonaill, and the rest of the fugitives, 1608, TNA, SP 63/223/8.

3 N. Canny, *Making Ireland British* (Oxford, 2001), p. 205.

4 Conditions of settling certain lands in Donegal, 20 Aug. 1610, *Tudor and Stuart proclamations*, ii, pp 19–20.

5 *ODNB* 38, p. 841; G. Hill (ed.), *The Montgomery manuscripts, 1603–1706* (Belfast, 1869), pp 11–12, 17.

6   *ODNB* 14, pp 658–60.

7   K. Brown, *Bloodfeud in Scotland, 1573–1625* (Edinburgh, 2003), pp 85–105.

8   Ibid., p. 93.

9   G. Hill, *An historical account of the plantation in Ulster* (Belfast, 1877), pp 294–5.

10 M. Perceval-Maxwell, *The Scottish migration to Ulster in the reign of James I* (London, 1973), pp 337–8.

11 *ODNB* 52, p. 196.

12 *ODNB* 39, pp 942–3.

13 *ODNB* 32, pp 5–6.

14 S. Adams, 'James VI and the politics of south-west Scotland, 1603–1625', in J. Goodare and M. Lynch (eds), *The reign of James VI* (Edinburgh, 2000), pp 228–40; J. Goodare, *The government of Scotland, 1560–1625* (Oxford, 2004).

15 Hill, *An historical account of the plantation in Ulster*, pp 293–5.

16 Ibid., p. 296.

17 *Irish Patent Rolls of James I*, p. 29.

18 Hill, *An historical account of the plantation in Ulster*, pp 327–9.

19 Walter McSweeney's genealogy has been preserved in the Ó Cléirigh Book of Genealogies: See P. Walsh (ed.), *Leabhar Chlainne Suibhne* (Dublin, 1920), p. 115.

20 Hill, *An historical account of the plantation in Ulster*, pp 328–9.

21 Ibid., p. 329.

22 Byrne (ed.), *A history of Ireland*, p. 121.

23 The bishop of Limerick to Sir Arthur Chichester, 3 June 1610, TNA, SP 63/229/49; *Irish Patent Rolls of James I*, p. 175.

24 Perceval-Maxwell, *The Scottish migration to Ulster*, p. 359.

25 Ibid., pp 360–1.

26 Hill, *An historical account of the plantation in Ulster*, pp 323–6;

27 *Patent Rolls of James I*, p. 268.

28 Ibid., p. 293.

29 Sir Arthur Chichester to the privy council, 12 Sept. 1608, TNA, SP 63/225/184.

30 Lord Chancellor of Ireland to my Lord, 8 Aug. 1608, TNA, SP 63/224/249.

31 Lord Deputy and council to the lords of the council, 30 Sept. 1605, TNA, SP 63/217/154.

32 P. Walsh, *Gleanings from Irish manuscripts* (Dublin, 1918), pp 29–30, 34, 39, 40, 44.

33 Ambassador William Trumbull to King James I, 7 Apr. 1614, TNA, SP 77/11/f. 27–9.

34 Ambassador William Trumbull to the British Secretary of State, 9 June 1615, TNA, SP 77/11/f. 341.

35 B. Jennings, 'The career of Hugh, son of Rory O'Donnell, earl of Tirconnell, in the Low Countries, 1607–1642', *Studies* 30 (1941), 226.

36 Ambassador William Trumbull to King James I, 7 Apr. 1614, TNA, SP 77/11/f. 27–9.

37 List of the principal persons who are going to Spain with the earl of Tír Chonaill, 8 Nov. 1607, given in M. Kerney Walsh, "*Destruction by peace*": *Hugh O'Neill after Kinsale* (Monaghan, 1986), pp 184–5.

38 The bishop of Limerick to Sir Arthur Chichester, 3 June 1610, TNA, SP 63/229/49.

39 McGettigan, *Red Hugh O'Donnell*, pp 129–33.

40 *Inquis. Rot.*, ii, 7 Apr. 1632.

41 Bishop Andrew Knox to the lord justices of Ireland, 26 Apr. 1632, TNA, SP 63/253/143.

42 'A survey of the present estate of the plantations in the counties of Donegal and Londonderry, taken by Sir Thomas Phillips, knight, and Richard Hadsor, esquire, anno 1622', V. Treadwell (ed.), *The Irish commission of 1622* (Dublin, 2006), pp 620–1.

43 Ibid., p. 622.

44 Canny, *Making Ireland British*, p. 196; Perceval-Maxwell, *The Scottish migration to Ulster*, pp 26–7.

45 Release from Sir Archibald Atcheson to John Murray, earl of Annandale, of his rights to the great proportion of the Rosses and other lands in Co. Donegal, 6 Aug. 1632, British Library, Add Charter 7051.

46 Perceval-Maxwell, *The Scottish migration to Ulster*, pp 171–4.

47 R. Simington (ed.), *The Civil Survey, 1654–1656, Counties of Donegal, London-Derry and Tyrone*, vol. iii (Dublin, 1937), p. 72.

48 Treadwell, *Irish commission*, pp 610–11.

49 Ibid., p. 611.

50 Ibid., p. 612.

51 Abstract of diverse papers concerning Ireland, 1623, TNA, SP 63/241/404.

52 James, Lord Balfour of Clonawley to John, earl of Annandale, 20 July 1626, *Laing MSS*, i, pp 169–72.

53 Simington (ed.), *The Civil Survey 1654–1656, County Donegal*, pp 72–6.

54 The king to the lord deputy, 28 Feb. 1629, *SP Dom.*, i, pp 405–6.

55 The king to the lord deputy, 3 June 1629, *SP Dom.*, i, p. 438.
56 Hill, *An historical account of the plantation in Ulster*, p. 323.
57 Treadwell, *Irish commission*, p. 616.
58 Ibid., p. 617.
59 Ibid., pp 617–18.
60 Ibid., p. 618.
61 Ibid., p. 622.
62 Hill, *An historical account of the plantation in Ulster*, p. 523.
63 Treadwell, *Irish commission*, p. 619; Brian Lacey et al. (eds), *Archaeological survey of County Donegal* (Lifford, 1983), pp 367–9.
64 Simington (ed.), *The Civil Survey 1654–1656*, iii, pp 134–7; K. McKenny, 'British Settler society in Donegal, *c*.1625–1685', in W. Nolan et al. (eds), *Donegal: history and society* (Dublin, 1995), p. 340.
65 Treadwell, *Irish Commission*, p. 617; Hill, *An historical account of the plantation in Ulster*, p. 527.
66 *A survey of the present estate of the plantations*, p. 618.
67 Ibid., p. 619.
68 Information from Donal O'Donnell of Glenties to John O'Donovan, 1835, *Ordnance Survey Letters Donegal* (unpublished appendix), p. 90.
69 Hill, *An historical account of the plantation in Ulster*, p. 523.
70 Ibid., pp 526–7.
71 R. Hunter, 'Plantation in Donegal', in Nolan et al. (eds), *Donegal: history and society*, pp 318–19; B. Mac Cuarta, *Catholic revival in the north of Ireland, 1603–41* (Dublin, 2007), p. 107.
72 A copy of an examination taken by my Lord Deputy and our Sergeant Brerton, 11 Oct. 1628, TNA, SP 63/247/180; Mac Cuarta, *Catholic revival in the north of Ireland*, p. 100.
73 Treadwell, *Irish commission*, p. 622.
74 Extract of a letter from Sir William Stewart dated 21 October 1628 at Acheenteen unto the Lord Deputy and received at Dublin the 26th of the same, TNA, SP 63/247/206.
75 L. McKenna (ed.), *Iomarbhagh na bhfileadh – the contention of the bards* (London, 1918); J. Leerssen, *The contention of the bards (Iomarbhagh na bhFileadh) and its place in Irish political and literary history* (London, 1994).
76 B. Cunningham, *O'Donnell histories: Donegal and the Annals of the Four Masters* (Rathmullan, 2007), pp 5–9.
77 E. Bhreathnach and B. Cunningham (eds), *Writing Irish history: the four masters and their world* (Dublin, 2007), pp 26–8.
78 P. Walsh, *Irish men of learning* (Dublin, 1947), pp 179–205.
79 J. McErlean, 'Eoin Ó Cuileannáin, bishop of Raphoe, 1625–1661', *Archivium Hibernicum*, 1 (Dublin, 1912), 77–121.
80 Ibid., pp 92 and 111.
81 Petition signed by Cormac O'Neill, Niall O'Donnell and Neachtan O'Donnell to the king, May 1621, *HMC Part I, Report and Appendix* (London, 1874), p. 277; Niall O'Donnell to Lord Deputy Chichester, 9 Oct. 1613, Philad. Papers, iv, p. 329; The names of the tenants of Sir Niall O'Donnell, and the number of 40 in-calf cows imposed upon them, Ibid., p. 331.
82 Lord Deputy of Ireland to Mr Secretary Conway, 31 May 1624, TNA, SP 63/238PT2/24.
83 NLI MS G488, p. 12.
84 L. McKenna, *Aithdioghluim Dána* (2 vols, Dublin, 1939) i, pp 97–9; ii, pp 25–6; Walsh, *Gleanings from Irish manuscripts*, pp 27–52.
85 Jennings, 'The career of Hugh, son of Rory O'Donnell', pp 229–32.
86 L. McKenna, *Dioghluim Dána* (Dublin, 1938), pp 307–12, 468.
87 NLI MS G488, p. 1.
88 For example see the address from Pope Urban VIII around this time, VL Barberini Lat. MS 2197, f. 1.
89 Letter of Hugh O'Donnell, earl of Tír Chonaill, 29 July 1630, Franciscan MS, UCD Archives, MS D.2, f. 151; Letter concerning personal matters, Maria Stuart O'Donnell, 4 Mar. 1631, VL Barberini Lat. MS 8620, f. 15.
90 J. Casway, 'Mary Stuart O'Donnell', *Donegal Annual*, 39 (1987), 28–38; *DIB* 7, pp 389–90.
91 Short annals of Tír Chonaill, *BAR*, II, pp 90–1.

2. THE REVOLT OF 1641

1 Abstract of diverse papers concerning Ireland, 1623, TNA, SP 63/241/399.
2 Ibid.
3 T. Ó Fiaich, 'Republicanism and separatism in the seventeenth century', *Léachtaí Cholm Cille* II (1971), pp 74–87;

Óscar Recio Morales, 'Florence Conry's memorandum for a military assault on Ulster, 1627', *Archivium Hibernicum*, 56 (2002), 65–72; T. O'Connor, 'Perfidious Machiavellian friar': Florence Conry's campaign for a Catholic Restoration in Ireland, 1592–1616', *Seanchas Ard Mhacha*, 19 (2002), 91–105; B. Hazard, *Faith and patronage: the political career of Flaithrí Ó Maolchonaire c.1560–1629* (Dublin, 2010).

4　Letters out of Ireland abstracted, 3 Mar. 1627, TNA, SP 63/245/299.

5　Lord Deputy of Ireland to the Lord Viscount Killultagh [abstracts], 29 Apr. 1627, TNA, SP 63/244/228.

6　McErlean, 'Eoin Ó Cuileannain', p.80.

7　See also Mac Cuarta, *Catholic revival in the North of Ireland*, p. 95.

8　Kerney Walsh, *"Destruction by Peace"*: *Hugh O'Neill after Kinsale*, pp 213, 270.

9　The examination of Nicholas Notary taken the 28 August 1628, concerning Turlough Roe O'Boyle, TNA, SP 63/247/118.

10　Extract of a letter from Sir William Stewart dated 21 October 1628 at Acheenteen unto the Lord Deputy and received at Dublin the 26th of the same, TNA, SP 63/247/206.

11　R. Gillespie, *Conspiracy: Ulster plots and plotters in 1615* (Belfast, 1987).

12　Lacey et al. (eds), *Archaeological Survey of Co. Donegal*, pp 376–9.

13　K. McKenny, *The Laggan army in Ireland, 1640–1685* (Dublin, 2005), p. 34.

14　Funeral certificate of Donal Gorm McSweeney, 4 June 1638, NLI, Genealogical Office Manuscript 70/120.

15　Walsh (ed.), *LCS*, pp xxxi–xxxii, xxxv, xl.

16　Examination of Henry Cartan, Quartermaster of Colonel Owen O'Neill's regiment in Flanders, 12 Feb. 1642, in J. Gilbert (ed.), *A contemporary history of affairs in Ireland* (Dublin, 1879) i, p. 396.

17　Annalistic note by Mícheál Ó Cléirigh written in his copy of the Martyrology of Donegal, given in J. O'Donovan, 'The O'Donnells in exile', *Duffy's Hibernian Magazine*, 1 (1860), p. 7.

18　R. Stradling, *The Spanish monarchy and Irish mercenaries: the Wild Geese in Spain, 1618–68* (Dublin, 1994), pp 26–7.

19　Ibid., p. 126.

20　Ibid., pp 115–16.

21　Annalistic note by Mícheál Ó Cléirigh, *Duffy's Hibernian Magazine*, 1 (1860), p. 7.

22　Deposition of Mulrony Carroll, *Depositions in the County of Donegal*, TCD MS 839, f. 125.

23　Copy of a letter of Everden McSweeney, Justice of Peace in the kingdom of Ireland, 27 Oct. 1641, TNA, SP 63/260/141.

24　Deposition of Ann Dutton, *Depositions in the County of Donegal*, TCD MS 839, f. 126; Deposition of John Ravenscourt, Ibid, f. 128.

25　Deposition of Mulrony Carroll, Deposition of Ann Dutton, *Depositions in the County of Donegal*, TCD MS 839, f. 125 and f. 126.

26　Deposition of Mulrony Carroll, *Depositions in the County of Donegal*, TCD MS 839, f. 125.

27　Deposition of Ann Dutton, *Depositions in the County of Donegal*, TCD MS 839, f. 126.

28　Deposition of Mulrony Carroll, *Depositions in the County of Donegal*, TCD MS 839, f. 125.

29　Deposition of Ann Dutton, *Depositions in the County of Donegal*, TCD MS 839, f. 126.

30　Deposition of Mulrony Carroll, *Depositions in the County of Donegal*, TCD MS 839, f. 125.

31　Letter of Everden McSweeney, 27 Oct. 1641, TNA, SP 63/260/141.

32　Deposition of James Kennedy, *Depositions in the County of Donegal*, TCD MS 839, f. 127.

33　Deposition of Mulrony Carroll, *Depositions in the County of Donegal*, TCD MS 839, f. 125.

34　Deposition of James Kennedy, *Depositions in the County of Donegal*, TCD MS 839, f. 127.

35　Deposition of Ann Dutton, *Depositions in the County of Donegal*, TCD MS 839, f. 126; Simington (ed.), *The Civil Survey 1654–1656, Co. Donegal*, p. 107.

36　Deposition of Christopher Parmenter, *Depositions in the County of Donegal*, TCD MS 839, f. 132.

37　Deposition of John Ravenscourt, *Depositions in the County of Donegal*, TCD MS 839, f. 128.

38　Fragment, *Depositions in the County of Donegal*, TCD MS 839, f. 126.

39　Fragment, *Depositions in the County of Donegal*, TCD MS 839, f. 127.

40 Letter of Everden McSweeney, 27 Oct. 1641, TNA, SP 63/260/141; Craebhscaoileadh Cloinne Dálaigh in *BAR*, II, pp 196–9.

41 McKenny, *The Laggan army in Ireland*, p. 40.

42 Relation by Colonel Audley Mervyn, 1642, in Gilbert (ed.), *Contemporary history*, ii, p. 465.

43 *ODNB* (52), pp 746–7.

44 Relation by Colonel Audley Mervyn, in Gilbert (ed.), *Contemporary history*, ii p. 470.

45 Petition of Lieutenant Colonel Audley Mervyn to the Lords and other commissioners for Irish affairs, 1642, *Appendix: the manuscripts of the house of lords, HMC Report 5*, p. 65.

46 Relation by Colonel Audley Mervyn, in Gilbert (ed.), *Contemporary history*, pp 466–7.

47 Ibid., p. 470.

48 Deposition of Ann Dutton, *Depositions in the County of Donegal*, TCD MS 839, f. 126.

49 McKenny, *The Laggan Army*, p. 44.

50 Relation by Colonel Audley Mervyn, in Gilbert (ed.), *Contemporary history*, ii pp 471–2.

51 W. Harkin, *Scenery and antiquities of northwest Donegal* (Derry, 1893), pp 71–5; N. Ó Dónaill, *Na Glúnta Rosannacha* (Dublin, 1974), pp 111–14.

52 Harkin, *Scenery and antiquities*, p. 72; Ó Dónaill, *Na Glúnta Rosannacha*, p. 112.

53 Relation by Colonel Audley Mervyn, in Gilbert (ed.), *Contemporary history*, pp 472–3; McKenny, *The Laggan army*, pp 42–3.

54 Relation by Colonel Audley Mervyn, in Gilbert (ed.), *Contemporary history*, ii p. 472.

55 C. Dillon (ed.), 'Cín Lae Uí Mhealláin, Friar O Meallan Journal', in C. Dillon and H. Jefferies (eds) *Tyrone: history and society* (Dublin, 2000), p. 342.

56 Relation by Colonel Audley Mervyn, in Gilbert (ed.), *Contemporary history*, p. 473.

57 Short Annals of Tír Chonaill, *BAR*, II, pp 90–1; Dillon (ed.), *Cín Lae Uí Mhealláin*, p. 342; Relation by Colonel Audley Mervyn, in Gilbert (ed.), *Contemporary history*, ii p. 473; Colonel Henry O'Neill's journal, in Gilbert (ed.), *Contemporary history*, vi, p. 197.

58 Aphorismical discovery of treasonable faction, in Gilbert (ed.), *Contemporary history*, i, pp 42–3.

59 Dillon (ed.), 'Cín Lae Uí Mhealláin', p. 343.

60 Statement by Sir William Stewart, 12 Oct. 1643, in Gilbert (ed.), *Contemporary history*, ii, pp 552–3.

61 'A brief and methodical relation of the most cruel and tyrannical persecution which the most revered and zealous prelate, the Lord Bishop of Raphoe, John O'Cullinane, suffered in Ireland of late', in P. Moran (ed.), *Spicilegium Ossoriense: being a collection of original letters and papers illustrative of the history of the Irish church from the reformation to the year 1800*, (3 vols, Dublin, 1874), i pp 304–5.

62 Aphorismical discovery of treasonable faction, in Gilbert (ed.), *Contemporary history*, i, p. 49; Dillon (ed.), 'Cín Lae Uí Mhealláin', p. 351.

63 Account of the battle of Benburb by a British officer of Sir John Clotworthy's regiment, in Gilbert, (ed.), *Contemporary history*, ii, p. 686.

64 *The manuscripts of the house of lords, Appendix, HMC Report 5*, Order Aug. 14 1643, p. 101; Order Apr. 5 1643, p. 79.

65 M. Ó Siochrú, *Confederate Ireland, 1642–1649* (Dublin, 1999), p. 258.

66 NLI MS Q488, p. 8.

67 Aphorismical discovery of treasonable faction, in Gilbert (ed.), *Contemporary history*, i, p. 118.

68 An anonymous note of Ulster regiments which will submit to the king [Ulster business] 1648, Gilbert (ed.), *Contemporary history*, ii, pp 759–60.

69 Daniel O'Neill to Ormond, 6 Oct. 1649, in Gilbert (ed.), *Contemporary history*, iv, p. 294; Articles between Ormond and Owen O'Neill, 20 Oct. 1649, Ibid., p. 300.

70 Confederate Commissioners to Ormond – Concerning Hugh Boy O'Donnell's men, 9 Feb. 1649, in Gilbert (ed.), *Contemporary history*, ii, p. 767.

71 E. Mac Cárthaigh, 'Marbhna ar Aodh Buidhe Ó Domhnaill (1649)', *Ériu*, 50 (1999), 53–4, 60.

72 McKenny, *The Laggan army in Ireland*, pp 87–108.

73 Ibid., p. 85.

74 'Captain Henry Finch's relation of the siege of Londonderry, by the Scotch, Irish and disaffected English, 1649', in Gilbert (ed.), *Contemporary history*, iv, p. 440.

75 Ibid., pp 440–1; W. Kelly, 'The forgotten siege of Derry, March-August, 1649', in W. Kelly (ed.), *The sieges of Derry* (Dublin, 2001), p. 40.

76 Captain Henry Finch's relation, in Gilbert (ed.), *Contemporary history*, iv, p. 445.
77 Commission to Colonel Mulmurry McSweeney, 23 Dec. 1649, in Gilbert, *Contemporary history*, iv, p. 470.
78 J. Casway, 'The Belturbet Council and election of March 1650', *Clogher Record*, 12 (1986), pp 159–70.
79 Proclamation of the Bishop of Clogher, 20 May 1650, in Gilbert, *Contemporary history*, iv, pp 418–19.
80 D. O'Carroll, 'The battle of Scariffhollis', in L. Ronayne (ed.), *The battle of Scariffhollis* (Donegal, 2001), pp 45–53.
81 Aphorismical discovery, Gilbert (ed.), *Contemporary history*, iii, p. 88.
82 Colonel Henry O'Neill's Journal, in Gilbert (ed.), *Contemporary history*, vi, p. 213.
83 Declaration of the Ulster party, 20 May 1650, in Gilbert (ed.), *Contemporary history*, iv, p. 420.
84 *AFM*, vi, p. 2398.
85 M. Ó Siochrú, *God's executioner: Oliver Cromwell and the conquest of Ireland* (London, 2008), pp 192–220.
86 Captain Humffelsteed to Mr Blackbourne from aboard the Marigold in Killybegs, 29 Mar. 1653, TNA, SP 63/283/17.
87 P. Ó Gallachair, 'Tirconaill in 1641', in T.O'Donnell (ed.), *Father John Colgan OFM 1592–1658* (Dublin, 1959), pp 89, 108–10; Ó Dónaill, *Na Glúnta Rosannacha*, p. 114.
88 An Act for the settling of Ireland, 12 Aug. 1652, in Gilbert (ed.), *Contemporary history*, vi, p. 343.
89 R. Dunlop, *Ireland under the Commonwealth being a selection of documents relating to the Government of Ireland From 1651 to 1659*, (2 vols Manchester, 1913), i p. 246. (See also p. 263 for documents: The ensuing letter, superscribed to Commissary General Reynolds and Colonel Venables, 4 Aug. 1652; Ordered Head Money be offered for the following traitors, 23. Aug. 1652, Colonel Mulmurry McSweeney £100).
90 Simington (ed.), *The Civil Survey 1654–1656, Co. Donegal*, p. 114.

3. CONFISCATION AND RESTORATION
BUT A SECOND 'TIMES OF TROUBLE'

1 'Sir Thomas Powys (for Petitioner)', 13 Feb. 1692, Cunningham v Sir R.

Creighton, alias Murray, *HMC, 13th Report, Appendix, Part V* (London, 1892), p. 489.
2 Simington (ed.), *The Civil Survey, 1654–1656, Co. Donegal*, pp 98, 103 and 107.
3 Ibid., p. 23.
4 Ibid., p. 88.
5 Ibid. pp 129–37.
6 Ibid., pp 130 and 137.
7 Ibid., pp 104–7.
8 'A seventeenth-century Letterkenny manuscript', *Donegal Annual*, 3 (1956), 139–40.
9 *AFM*, vi, p. 2390.
10 Letter of an Irish priest, 23 Aug. 1701, in J. O'Donovan, 'The O'Donnells in exile', *Duffy's Hibernian Magazine*, 2 (Aug. 1860), 3 (Sept. 1860), p. 106.
11 *AFM*, vi, pp 2400–1.
12 Mac Erlean, 'Eoin Ó Cuileannáin, bishop of Raphoe, 1625–1661', p. 80; Rosa O'Doherty the widow of General O'Neill also died in Brussells in 1660. Mary O'Donnell, a sister of Red Hugh and Rory O'Donnell died in 1662; see *DIB* 7, pp 355–6 and *BAR*, II, pp 126–36.
13 The humble petition of Colonel Mulmurry McSweeney, Dec. 1660, TNA, SP 63/305/34.
14 List attached to Colonel Mulmurry McSweeney's petition, Dec. 1660, TNA, SP 63/305/36.
15 The humble petition of Colonel Mulmurry McSweeney, Dec. 1660, TNA, SP 63/305/34.
16 *CSPI* 1660–2, p. 694; Ibid., 1663–5, p. 53.
17 Government decision on Colonel Mulmurry McSweeney's petition, 10 Dec. 1660, TNA, SP 63/305/35.
18 Dunlop, *Ireland under the Commonwealth*, p. 246; Simington (ed.), *The Civil Survey 1654–56*, iii, p. 135; List attached to Colonel Mulmurry McSweeney's petition, 1660, TNA, SP 63/305/36.
19 G. Tallon (ed.), *Court of Claims: submission and evidence 1663* (Dublin, 2006), p. xi.
20 The Catholic Declaration, 25 Mar. 1666, TNA, SP 63/320/160.
21 *HMC, 13th Rep.*, p. 488.
22 Ibid., p. 491.
23 G. Kirkham, '"No more to be got off the cat but the skin": management, landholding and economic change on the Murray of Broughton estate, 1670–1755', in Nolan et al. (eds), *Donegal: history and society*, p. 358.

24 HMC, *13th Rep.*, p. 488. For the relationship of the Murrays of Broughton to the Cunninghams of Mount Charles see the series of letters from Sir Albert's son Henry to Lady Broughton and John Murray preserved in the Meade Papers. For example: Henry Cunningham to Lady Broughton, 6 Nov. 1700, Meade Papers, NLI PC 679, Folder 1; see also: Sir Albert Cunningham to Richard Murray of Broughton, 10 Dec. 1687, PRONI, D2860/1/3.

25 HMC, *13th Rep.*, p. 489.

26 Ibid., p. 491; Sir Albert Cunningham to Richard Murray of Broughton, 10 Dec. 1687, PRONI, D2860/1/3.

27 HMC, *13th Rep.,* p. 489.

28 Kirkham, 'Management, landholding and economic change on the Murray of Broughton estate', p. 357; Henry Cunningham to John Murray, 23 July 1701 Meade Papers, NLI PC 679, Folder 1; Henry Cunningham to John Murray, 26 July 1702, Meade Papers, NLI PC 679, Folder 1.

29 Henry Cunningham to Lady Broughton, 21 Nov. 1694, Meade Papers, NLI PC 679, Folder 1.

30 *NHI*, 9, p. 353; Letter of Luke Plunkett, vicar general of Raphoe, 1 Nov. 1671, in Moran (ed.), *Spicilegium Ossoriense*, ii, p. 213.

31 NLI MS G488, p. 8.

32 The will of Hugh O'Donnell, earl of Tír Chonaill, 9 Apr. 1674, in O'Donovan 'The O'Donnells in exile', p. 110.

33 King Charles II to the lord deputy of Ireland, Richard, earl of Arran. 12 June 1684, TNA, SP 63/340/30.

34 Copy of the humble petition of Sir Albert Cunningham, knight, Lieutenant General of your majesty's ordnance in Ireland, PRONI, D2860/1/6.

35 W. King, *The state of the Protestants of Ireland under the late King James' Government* (London, 1692), Appendix No. 8, Lord Lieutenants and Deputy Lieutenants of Counties, p. 322.

36 Ibid.; J. Dalton, *King James' Irish army list* (Limerick, 1997), pp 34, 552.

37 The will of Hugh O'Donnell, earl of Tír Chonaill, 9 Apr. 1674, in O'Donovan, 'The O'Donnells in exile', p. 110; *King James' Irish army list*, pp 548–9.

38 M. Herity, 'The return of the Cathach to Ireland: conflicting accounts of the repatriation of the Cathach from the continent', in A. Smyth (ed.) *Seanchas: studies in early and medieval Irish archaeology, history and literature in honour of Francis J. Byrne* (Dublin, 2000), pp 454–5.

39 *DIB* 7, p. 371.

40 King, *The state of the Protestants of Ireland*, pp 327–8.

41 *A narrative of the siege of Londonderry by John Mackenzie* (London, 1690), p. 3.

42 Sir Albert Cunningham to Sir Henry Bollasis, 29 Aug. 1691, TCD MS 749/11/1065; (This regiment, the Inniskillen Dragoons, is still in existence, albeit in modified form, in the British army); An account of what subsistence the officers and private men of Sir Albert Cunningham's regiment of dragoons their record, Oct. 1690, British Library, Add. MS 29879.

43 *DIB* 9, pp 83–4.

44 The manuscripts of the house of lords, 15 June, 1689, *HMC 12th Report, Appendix, Part VI* (London, 1889), p. 142.

45 J. Simms, 'County Donegal in the Jacobite War (1688–91)', *Donegal Annual,* 7 (1967), p. 219.

46 J. Simms, *Jacobite Ireland* (London, 1969), p. 107; J. Miller, *James II* (New Haven, 1978), p. 227.

47 Simms, 'County Donegal in the Jacobite War', p. 220.

48 King, *The state of the Protestants of Ireland*, Appendix, p. 8.

49 Lacey et al. (eds), *Archaeological survey of County Donegal*, p. 378.

50 Simms, *Jacobite Ireland*, p. 165; D. Ó hÓgáin, *Myth, legend and romance: an encyclopaedia of the Irish folk tradition* (London, 1990), pp 337–8.

51 Ó hÓgáin, *Myth, legend and romance*, p. 337.

52 Letter of an Irish priest, 23 Aug. 1701, O'Donovan, 'The O'Donnells in exile', pp 53–4; B. Hazard, 'The manifesto of Field Marshal [recté: Colonel] Hugh O'Donnell, in justification of his departure from the kingdom without leave from Charles II, king of Spain, c.1690', *Irish Sword*, 104 (2008), 129–37.

53 Hazard, 'The manifesto of Field Marshal Hugh O'Donnell', pp 132–5.

54 O'Donovan, 'The O'Donnells in exile', p. 107.

55 Ibid., p. 56.

56 General Ginkel to the king, 8 Aug. 1691, *Calendar of state papers domestic, William and Mary 1690–1691* (London, 1898), p. 475.

57   Sir Albert Cunningham to Sir Henry
     Bollasis, 29 Aug. 1691, TCD MS
     749/11/1065.
58   Sir Albert Cunningham to Sir Henry
     Bollasis, 4 Sept. 1691, TCD MS
     749/11/1089.
59   H. Gorges for Captain Montgomery, 5
     Sept. 1691, TCD MS 749/11/1097.
60   Ibid.; Rob. Jekkins for Lieutenant
     Colonel Eiklin, 9 Sept. 1691, TCD MS
     749/11/1121.
61   Proclamation of the reward for the arrest
     of certain outlaws, 10 Dec. 1694, No. 1304,
     Tudor and Stuart proclamations, ii, p. 160.
62   Daniel O'Donnell had the Cathach
     repaired in 1723. (He 'refurbished the
     age-worn silver case'). Before he died in
     1735 Daniel left instructions that 'it should
     be given up to the chief of the name
     when applied for': Herity, 'The return of
     the Cathach to Ireland', pp 454–5; In 1709
     Daniel O'Donnell had a confirmation of
     arms issued to him by the Athlone Herald
     at the Jacobite Court: N. Kissane (ed.),
     Treasures from the National Library of Ireland
     (Dublin, 1994), pp 224–5.
63   R. Ó Cochlain, 'Hugh O'Donnell of
     Larkfield', *Donegal Annual,* 37 (1985), 46–7.

CONCLUSION

1   D. Dickson, 'Derry's backyard: the
     barony of Inishowen, 1650–1800', in
     Nolan et al. (eds), *Donegal: history and
     society*, p. 411.
2   Simms, 'County Donegal in the Jacobite
     War', pp 213–16.
3   Henry Cunningham to John Murray of
     Broughton, 15 Mar. 1701, Meade Papers,
     NLI PC 679, Folder 1.
4   Lady Cunningham to Alexander Murray
     of Broughton, 5 Jan. 1706, PRONI,

D2860/9/10; Major-General Henry
Cunningham to Alexander Murray of
Broughton, 11 Nov. 1704, PRONI,
D2860/5/23.
5   James Hamilton to Alexander Murray of
     Broughton, 4 Feb. 1729, PRONI,
     D2860/12/21.
6   James Hamilton to Alexander Murray of
     Broughton, 11 July 1729, PRONI,
     D2860/12/22.
7   Herity (ed.), *Ordnance Survey letters
     Donegal,* pp 45–6.
8   Genealogy of Jacobus O Friell [James
     O'Friel], October 1744, Genealogical
     Office Manuscript 162, f. 24 and f. 25
     Latin note.
9   Herity (ed.), *Ordnance Survey letters
     Donegal,* pp 25–7.
10   Major General Henry Cunningham to
     Alexander Murray of Broughton, 11
     Nov. 1704, PRONI, D2860/5/23.
11   James Hamilton to Alexander Murray of
     Broughton, 4 Feb. 1729, PRONI,
     D2860/12/21.
12   Fred. Hamilton to William King,
     Archbishop of Dublin, 9 Aug. 1715,
     Correspondence and Papers of William
     King, archbishop of Dublin, *Second
     Report of the Royal Commission on
     Historical Manuscripts* (London, 1874),
     Appendix to the second report,
     p. 251.
13   'Report on the state of Popery in Ireland
     in 1731', *Archivium Hibernicum* 1 (1912),
     pp 20–3.
14   Ibid, pp 20–1.
15   U. Bourke, *Sermons in Irish Gaelic by the
     most Revd James O'Gallagher* (Dublin,
     1878); *ODNB* (21), pp 311–12.
16   'Tit for Tat; or The Rater rated. A new
     Song, in way of Dialogue, between a
     Laggen Farmer and his Wife', in
     F. Ferguson (ed.), *Ulster Scots writing*
     (Dublin, 2008), p. 99.